THE
FISHERMAN'S
HANDBOOK

Distributed in Canada by Burns & MacEachern Limited, 62 Railside Road, Toronto, Canada

THE FISHERMAN'S HANDBOOK

*A Complete Guide to Fishing
in North America*

By
John Power
and
Jeremy Brown

Illustrated by E. B. Sanders

PAGURIAN PRESS

CHARLES SCRIBNER'S SONS
NEW YORK

A-3.72 (I)

Printed and Bound in Canada

Library of Congress Catalog Card Number: 70-385-29

SBN 684-12845-4

Contents

Introduction

THE FISHERMAN'S HANDBOOK is devoted to providing the latest, and most up-to-date information on fish, fishing skills and fishing locations.

It is a handbook that has been designed to provide a complete guide for the angler, whether he be a novice or a veteran of many fishing expeditions.

Our first chapter offers some useful information on precisely how to introduce a child to the delights of angling. Patience, tact and encouragement bring not only results for the child but a sense of accomplishment for the teacher.

Then we deal with the techniques of trolling, spin-casting, spinning, and that most elite of all methods, fly-fishing. You'll find a chapter on live bait, which offers a variety of proven methods to catch and keep the creatures which bridge the gap between hook and fish.

From years in the elements, we can offer some novel ideas about fishing gear, a much-neglected subject in fishing literature, but a subject which can not only improve comfort, but improve chances of landing that lunker.

Myths will never be completely erased, but in another chapter we review all the fishing lore, explain the origin of some fanciful beliefs, and provide from our experience which old and new beliefs hold water.

A section of this book which particularly excited our interest was the geographic distribution chart which follows the description of each fish. To our knowledge, this is the first work which has presented the information in this manner. Each state and province was asked to provide a detailed list of each species, whether it was abundant, or just present, or not available. Then we asked for the average size of each species, the state record, and when that record was attained. A quick glance at any chart will quickly show you where to find a particular fish, what size it normally attains, and what the record catch was for that location. We should caution the reader that these charts are as accurate as we could make them, but we are not responsible if errors were passed on to us through inadvertence by the many state and provincial officials who gave us enormous assistance.

No fishing book is complete without tips on what to do with fish after it's landed. This book tells readers not only how to keep the fish fresh, but offers a cooking section that gives advice on the best ways of preparing fish for the home as well as the hungry angler.

John Power
Jeremy Brown

Acknowledgements

The authors are indebted to a large number of state and provincial officials who contributed up-to-date information on records, new developments in stocking, and the availability of various fish. They are: Alabama, Charles D. Kelley, chief, Division of Game and Fish; Alaska, Rupert Andrews, director, Sports Fish Division; Arizona, Howard M. Bassett, chief, Fisheries; Arkansas, William H. Mathis, division chief, Fisheries; California, Alexander J. Calhoun, chief, Inland Fisheries; Colorado, Thomas M. Lynch, fish manager; Connecticut, Cole W. Wilde, chief, Fish Division; Delaware, officer of the director of Fish and Wildlife; Florida, John W. Woods, chief of Fisheries; Georgia, Leon Kirkland, chief of Fisheries; Idaho, James C. Simpson, chief, Fisheries; Illinois, William J. Harth, supervisor, Division of Fisheries; Indiana, Gene Bass, head, division of Fish and Game; Iowa, Harry M. Harrison, chief of Fish and Game; Kansas, Roy Schoonover, chief, Fisheries Division; Kentucky, Charles Bowers, director, Division of Fisheries; Louisiana, Joe L. Herring, chief, Fish and Game division; Maine, Lyndon W. Bond, chief, Fishery Research and Management Division; Maryland, Robert J. Rubelmann, chief, Fisheries Management; Massachusetts, James M. Shepard, director, Division of Fisheries, Michigan, William J. Mullendore, chief, information and education division; Minnesota, Richard Wettersten, director, Division of Game and Fish; Mississippi, Barry O. Freeman, chief of Fisheries; Missouri, Charles A. Purkett, Jr., chief, Fisheries; Montana, A. N. Whitney, chief, Fisheries management; Nebraska, Glen R. Foster, chief of Fisheries; Nevada, Thomas J. Trelease, chief of Fisheries; New Hampshire, Richard G. Seamans Jr., chief, Inland and Marine Fisheries; New Jersey, Robert A. Hayford, chief, Bureau of Fisheries Management; New Mexico, R. L. Brashears, chief, Fisheries; New York, Carl E. Parker, chief, Bureau of Fish; North Carolina, Joel

Arington; North Dakota, Dale L. Henegar, chief, Fishery Division; Ohio, Clayton Lakes, fish management section; Oklahoma, Ken Johnston, chief, Fisheries Division; Oregon, Jack Dugan, director, Information-Education; Pennsylvania, Arthur D. Bradford, chief, Fisheries Division; Rhode Island, Thomas J. Wright, chief, Fish and Wildlife; South Carolina, Pat Ryan, director, Game and Freshwater Fisheries; South Dakota, Robert Hanten, staff specialist, Fisheries; Tennessee, Hudson Nicols, chief, Fish Management; Texas, Marion Toole, Inland Fisheries; Utah, Don Andriano, chief, Fisheries Management; Vermont, Leonard C. Halnon, chief fish biologist; Virginia, Jack M. Hoffman, chief, Fish Division; Washington, Thor C. Tollefson, director, Fisheries; West Virginia, David W. Robinson, assistant chief, Fish Management; Wisconsin, Charles Lloyd, director Bureau of Fish Management; Wyoming, W. Donald Dexter, state fish warden.

In Canada, Alberta, Stuart B. Smith, fish and wildlife director; New Brunswick, Brian C. Carter, director, Fish and Wildlife Branch; Newfoundland, D. G. Pike, director of Wildlife; Nova Scotia, M. H. Prime, director, Wildlife Conservation division; Prince Edward Island, John Bain, director, Fish and Wildlife Division; Quebec, Bruce Bailey; Saskatchewan, Paul Naftel, superintendent of Fisheries; Yukon Territories, J. A. Summers, district conservation officer.

Our thanks to the Rock City Tobacco Co., who kindly permitted the text of How Hip Are Hypotheses?? to be reprinted from The Sportsman Guide to Canadian Fishing written by John Power.

The authors also gratefully acknowledge the heroic efforts of Brenna Brown in collating the information from the states and provinces, and Jean Power in typing and checking manuscripts, and keeping the show on the road.

Chapter 1

Anglers Are Made, Not Born

Blueprints for a bridge to span the generation gap are contained in your tackle box. And it's a fortunate fisherman who's handed an opportunity to teach his old tricks to a young lad. These lessons can be as rewarding for the professor as the pupil.

Hand-in-glove is the responsibility which comes when instilling opinions and attitudes on impressionable minds. Here's a golden opportunity to mold a mature outdoorsman who will view life as it is. With your help he will grow mentally tall and be above the ostrich-like escape from reality through drugs and pot.

However, you'll soon sour your budding buddy by saddling him with a bamboo pole and length of twine. No father would expect to develop a future hockey ace by strapping bob skates to his boy's boots, and the same principle applies to the fishing game. You'll rarely succeed in making him into a fisherman by handicapping a kid with shoddy equipment, or a discarded baitcasting rig which backlashed its way into the attic years ago.

The price tag on a decent starting outfit is no more than a moderate night on the town. Besides, it is an investment in his future, and skimping on tackle can be costly in the long run.

From the age of 10, most youngsters can handle an openface spinning reel. A dependable rod and reel combination will cost in the neighborhood of $25, and will likely give trouble-free performance for several years. When initiating a lad whose tiny fingers are unable to pick up the line or flip the bail without considerable difficulty, then give the nod to spin-casting gear.

Remember that a 7-foot spinning rod in the grasp of smallfry can be likened to an adult using one twice as long. Spin-casting rods are not only shorter than spinning wands, but their off-set handles are easier for half-pint hands to hang onto. Spincast reels require less dexterity to operate than do spinning models, and it's possible to purchase a reasonably reliable rod/reel/line combo for about $15.

The back yard is a good site for the initial lessons. Let the greenhorn get the hang of it by trying to drop a practice plug inside a bucket. This can be good fun, and will hone the keenness. Your boy or girl will be eager for a chance to test his or her newly-acquired skills where they really count. Following a few such practice sessions, the child will be able to lay out long and fairly accurate casts, and he'll find pleasure in doing so, even if the fish are uncooperative.

Nothing is less geared to the appetite of an eager kid than the boredom of waiting for a bobber to disappear beneath the surface. Don't load the child's reel with heavy unbreakable line. Once you exceed 8-pound test, you rob much of the pleasure which comes with ease of handling and ability to cast impressive distances. It's unrealistic to expect a line to last more than a portion of the season, regardless of quality.

Teach the newly-initiated to snap off the final few feet before each excursion, explaining how the tail-end loses its resiliency and strength through stretching and fraying. Kids are predictably "hung up" more frequently than veteran anglers. But don't make the child nervous over the prospect of losing a hook or lure. Keep in mind that most successful anglers leave a lot of "hardware" on lake and river bottoms. When you knock on the fish's lair, many lures get left on the doorstep.

The slipping clutch or "adjustable drag" will off-set a youngster's natural tendency to "horse" a fish to net as fast as he can crank the handle. One lesson a beginner must learn is that thrills, fun and excitement conclude once the quarry has been landed.

Outfit your youngster with his or her own tackle box filled with split shot, hooks, and a supply of inexpensive lures. Casting is only one facet in the art of fishing, and all of its intricacies cannot be jammed into a crash course. There are basic techniques such as pinching split shot on line, tying swivels, fastening hooks and affixing live bait. Lend your assistance and expertise only as long as it's needed. Emphasize independence.

When a lad is snagged, let him free it or break it without your help. And if he is too tiny to snap a solidly snagged monofilament line, show him the old bank fisherman's trick of wrapping it around his body, then turning until it gives.

Energetic children crave action, and enthusiasm is sustained with fish — regardless of size and species. Panfish neatly fill the beginner's bill — leave the pike and musky for later piscatorial pursuits.

Never take over the playing of a fish. When kids hook into a lunker they're inclined to panic and hand the rod to the old man. Encourage, advise, but never do battle. Teach that a successful outing is not dependent upon a heavy stringer, and it makes conservation sense to return a fish to grow and fight another day. Once you have kindled a love affair between your child and the great outdoors, its flame will be enduring. Book learning often leaves by the other ear, but what's taught in God's classroom stops in the middle.

The man who tutors a boy in fishing, hunting and love of nature won't receive instant remuneration for his time and efforts. With a small monetary investment, plus large doses of patience and guidance, your fledgling fisher will one day become your piscatorial partner.

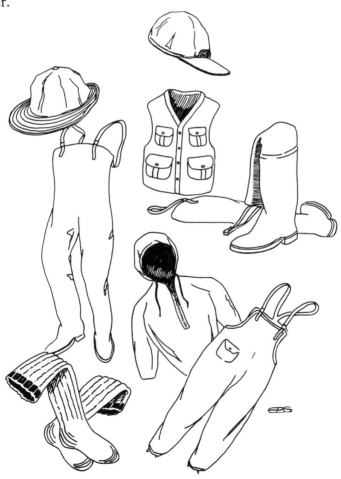

Chapter 2

Garbing For The Game

There are relatively few individuals who dress for this sport, and collectively they look like candidates for a soup line. It's not the cost. Paradoxically, bucks are no object when purchasing tackle or gear. Nor do fishermen recoil at the thoughts of digging deep to finance a flight promising fabulous fishing at its termination. Anglers should doff their impractical apparel and don sensible attire.

The correct headwear is of prime importance. It's tough to top a wide-brimmed felt fedora, siliconed to make it shower-proof. It will breathe and be more comfortable when the sweatband and lining are removed. In hot weather, periodically dip it in the drink. The evaporation principle keeps fishermen coolheaded, just as it does with the contents of a felt-covered canteen. Some prefer straw bonnets or caps with a lengthy peak.

Those who have long been plagued by black flies, mosquitoes, and other biting, boring, bloodsucking insects might find this scourge is minimized by a change of clothing. It's a proven fact that light-colored fabrics repel bugs, whereas darker tones attract them. Yellow, white and khaki are all okay, but it's thumbs down on maroon, black, brown and dark green.

Pack along a pair of rubber surgical gloves during black fly season. They'll effectively shield your skin against their attacks, and a fast swish in the water relieves the heat problem. Talcum powder will aid in getting them on.

Once a trout fisher wears a fishing vest he quickly discovers he can't get along without it. The best-designed garments have enough pockets to take all the fisherman's paraphenalia. And the external patch of sheepskin is ideal for holding hooks, flies or small lures. When purchasing a vest, check if it's cut to ride above waders. If your choice is a jacket in lieu of a vest, it should have bi-swing shoulders for ease in casting.

The average angler needs both chest-high waders and hip boots. Waders are the uniform for big rivers. They're also half-a-rainsuit and provide posterior protection when depositing your assets on the bank. Suspenders keep them up, but if negotiating swift waters, wear a belt around the outside which keeps the "dampness" out in the event of a splashdown.

Waders should have ample girth to encompass a warm jacket or quilted vest, and the feet should be commodious enough to accommoderate felt insoles plus two pairs of thick wool socks. A felt sole will give surer grip on slippery rocks, and a ribbed bottom lends stability on mud or clay. The waterproof fabric tops on both chest-highs and hip boots get top marks. They're light and virtually snag-proof.

In small streams and ponds, hip boots usually suffice. They should have an interior knee-harness, which takes strain off the belt. These are equipped with snap fasteners to secure the rolled-down tops when hiking overland. Summer or southern wading is often a trouser and sneaker proposition — a welcome respite.

Don't leave boots in a cottage, shed or car trunk during northern winters, or you'll hasten their demise. Roll them loosely and store where it's cool and dark.

Fair-weather fishermen miss out on some of the hottest action. The prudent enthusiast is always prepared for the worst, even if his rainwear is only a vinyl suit or coat which resides in the tackle box. The rubberized nylon suits get a widespread nod. But during strenuous activities, like portaging, they become as soaked inside from condensation and perspiration as they do on the outside from the rain.

Ponchos are great gear for boat and bank fishing, and can even double as a shelter in an emergency. Perhaps the best of all is the tough, tightly-woven cotton suit worn by mountain climbers. Unfortuanately, the price tag makes them prohibitive for most pocketbooks. Whatever your choice in rainware, ensure it's commodious enough to go over the extra clothing needed on chilly days.

Fishermen who are too smart to come in out of the cold usually have the wisdom to know what to wear when the north wind howls. For starters, fish-net or mesh longjohns are ideal, trapping insulating air between your clothing and your body. A wool turtleneck sweater is excellent, eliminating the need for a scarf. Wool has the unique feature of providing some warmth, even when wet. Add a feather-light insulated vest and you'll remain cosy on the chilliest days.

A warm hat is a curb for cold feet, so many sport a wollen toque or balaclava when the mercury dips near freezing. If the head and neck are comfortable, the body transmits excess heat to the extremities, which act as radiators. If Jack Frost is inclined to nip your fingers and toes, a hat or parka hood might alleviate your discomfort. Because it's awkward casting with heavy gloves, a handwarmer in the pocket will thaw numb fingers during periodic time-outs.

However, whether you wisely follow these guidelines or not, remember clothes don't make the man — nor the fisherman.

Streamer Fly

Dry Fly

Wet Fly

Chapter 3

Bait-Casting

Within hours an angler can be proficient with spinning tackle, a few days will turn a tyro into an accomplished fly caster, but years are needed to master the art of bait-casting.

Recent improvements and innovations have made great strides toward eliminating many of yesteryear's headaches. Fine lines, anti-backlash and drag devices, and glass rods have all contributed. Backlashes are the bait-caster's biggest bugbear. These insufferable "birdsnests" occur when the spool revolves faster than the line peels off, causing over-running to the tune of hair-curling prose.

The cursed backlash can be minimized, if not eliminated, by synchronizing thumb pressure on the spool. Thumbing can only be mastered through practice, patience, and familiarity with your outfit. Such factors as weight and shape of lure, thickness of line, wind direction, velocity and idiosyncracies of your reel must all be considered.

Most of today's better reels have excellent anti-backlash features, which go along way toward making them foulproof. A clutch or star-drag is also standard with many quality reels.

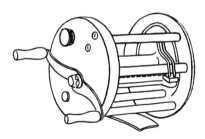

Silk, linen and even horsehair lines have given way to braided nylon, dacron and monofilament. The rule-of-thumb is to use as light a line as feasible, considering species and waters. A 10-pound test is adequate for most fishy pursuits, but if finny big-game is the order of the day, then a line doubling that strength is recommended.

The spool should be filled to near-capacity, and the simplest way is to install a cork or plastic arbour on the spindle. The standard 50-yard length will usually bring it to the desired level. The same end can be accomplished with the use of backing.

Since most lines come in two connecting spools, many fishermen — especially trollers — prefer to discard arbours and wind on as much of the 100-yards as their reel will handle. Devotees find they require a couple of reels, a lightweight model with fine line, and a heavy-duty type with weightier test. Remember, a light line won't coordinate with a heavy lure, nor will the opposite combination perform satisfactorily.

A factor few consider when buying a baitcasting reel is the gear ratio, which can vary from 2 to 1 to 4 to 1. This is mighty important if a fast retrieve is needed, as when plugging weedy, snag-riddled habitat. Also, check the level-wind device, which lays the line evenly over the spool.

The transition in outdoor gear has been as revolutionary as in our mode of travel. Fishing rods had their horse and buggy era too. Glass in your windows? . . . perhaps, but incomprehensible in angling poles, according to an 1860 sportsman's bible.

The author describes poles of "vine, bamboo, hazel and hickory some made to fit in canvas bags whilst others resemble walking sticks." The 19th century do-it-yourself'r was advised to "use crab trees for the stocks and hazel or yew switches for the tops. A whale-bone top is also an extremely good article and should have a strong loop of horsehair whipt on it." Furthermore, "a pike rod ought to be strong, stiff, and straight as a dart, and need never be more than 14-feet long."

Many a diehard guards a cherished metal foil he's fished with for umpteen years. It's questionable if even modern glass rods can surpass the wonderful way these steel rapiers respond. However, glass has lightness plus strength, and few will dispute the advantages of a hollowglass rod in the hands of an expert.

There are many sizes and weights, but try to balance your rod with your reel. A feather-light reel wound with lightweight line should be accompanied by an appropriate rod. Length varies according to the angler's favorite fish, but a 5-footer is a good average. Most bait-casting spoons and plugs weigh ½ to 1 ounce, with an average of ⅝-ounce.

Bait-casting tackle is made-to-order when plugging for lunker largemouths inhabiting lily and stump-clogged shorelines and inlets. Accuracy is another plus. An ace bait-caster will drop his lure on a dime, every time. Casting should be done with the reel handle up, and unless hampered by overhanging brush, the overhead cast is the safest, and most accurate.

Alter the speed of your retrieve — simple to do if you've a wide gear ratio.

Many fishermen fail to give fish credit for what is probably inherent wariness, rather than intelligence. In spite of the fact braided casting line can be easily spotted underwater, many merely affix an equally-apparent leader to their line. The answer lies in a 3-5 foot length of monofilament between line and lure.

Casting tackle was originally conceived in the 19th century for the purpose of casting live minnows. Live bait is still a winner, but today's tackle allows you to fling it farther with greater accuracy. Remember, it should be lobbed — not cast like "hardware."

This gear is A-1 for many trolling situations, particularly with star-drag equipment. Bait-casting is now riding on the crest of an unprecedented, unpredicted, but well-deserved resurgence in popularity.

Chapter 4

Spinning

Spinning tackle has revolutionized fishing, and anyone can now become an overnight casting expert. Timing is the only major hurdle, and once the moment of release has been mastered the lure lands on target.

It's been responsible for introducing legions of novices to the finest pastime in the world. Many such sportsmen might have otherwise wasted a lifetime of recreational hours venting, or creating, frustrations by trying to whack the beejeebers out of a little white ball.

The principle of spinning precludes possibility of the backlashes which have plagued bait-casters forever. The spool of the reel is simply a drum to hold the line. When casting, the weight of the bait or lure pulls the line off the stationary spool.

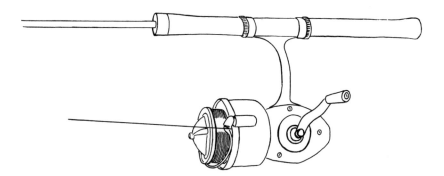

The lure is tossed by holding the line on the tip of the fore-finger, snapping the "bail" open, and dropping the finger at the correct moment during the cast. When the handle is cranked, the revolving bail flips over, picks up the line and winds it evenly back onto the spool.

Reels with larger spools have a faster retrieve. The speed of the rewind should be gauged by waters, lure or bait, species, and familiarity with the reel. Spinning reels are mounted on the underside of a straight-handle. The seat should be comfortably straddled with two fingers fore and two aft of the post.

The adjustable drag is a big plus, permitting the use of a "next-to-nothing" line, with little likelihood of breakage, providing the tension is correctly adjusted. The clutch control knob acts as the spool cap in most cases, although some models feature it at the rear of the housing, and on the crankshaft.

Pre-set the tension prior to your initial cast, ensuring it will "slip" by giving the line several sharp tugs. The adjustable drag allows the fish to run, but with a taut line's constant tiring pressure, until it finally succumbs to gaff or net.

All reels have an anti-reverse button — sometimes called a "click". Press it on when trolling or during the landing of fish. When engaged, it locks the crank so the handle can't spin if the adversary makes a run for it.

Don't wind when the creature on the other end of the line has ideas of heading elsewhere. Such tactics will result in twisted lines. Commence cranking again when the fish has stopped at the end of its run.

Give this fine piece of precision equipment the care it warrants and needs. Check under the spool for grit and chunks of monofilament which may be wrapped around the shaft as an aftermath of tangles. Replace the interior grease annually, and oil the crankshaft at frequent intervals. Keep a sharp eye for grooves on the bail's line roller. If you discover any, replace it before you flip another lure.

Gossamer lines are one of the most remarkable inventions, the development of which can be indirectly credited to spinning. These light lines follow a ¼-ounce lure a country mile, yet, when combined with a correctly tuned drag, stand up to the strain of a battling bruiser.

Too many load up with a line testing pounds more than required. This will defeat the pleasure and purpose of the game by shortening casts and fizzling fun. Four to 8 pound test is all the range required for freshwater fishers, with few exceptions.

Monofilament has captured the line market. A few prefer the limpness of braided nylon or dacron, but these lines haven't the durability, transparency, non-absorbency, or resistance to tangles inherent in monofilament. As line gets broken, the level on the spool lowers and the distance of casts shorten accordingly. Line should come to ⅛-1/16 inch from the lip of the spool. When it drops below that point it should be replaced.

One hundred yards will usually suffice, providing it's wound over backing in order to fill the spool. It's advisable to bring it to the edge of the lip when wound by hand. Then cast or troll it with a heavy weight attached. When rewound, the line will pack down compactly.

Certain lures and bait are inclined to twist monofilament. There are several ways to overcome this problem. A snap swivel or plastic keel will help combat twisting. So will the speed of your retrieve. Winding too rapidly makes a spoon spin instead of wobble, and causes the shank of a spinner to revolve. A twisted line can be made healthy again by letting it float downstream or stripping it out behind the boat.

Spinning rods come in a variety of lengths, weights and actions. The average freshwater wand is a medium-action 6½-footer. Most favor a tip action, with a hefty butt section tapering to a fine top. They're great for fast and accurate casting, while possessing power and backbone to control a finny heavyweight.

The limber, roll-action rod (called parabolique) is better suited to casting live bait. Almost all today's rods are hollow glass — lightweight, yet capable of absorbing a lot of use and abuse. Spinning rods have tapering guides to diminish the friction from the coils of line passing through them. Guides are an important feature to check when buying a rod. They should be agate or a very hard metal, such as stainless steel or carboloy.

Monofilament will quickly wear grooves in softer metals, which will then shred or nick the line. Those rods with fiberglass self-ferrules have a smoother action and are understandably lighter in weight than those connected by a metal joint.

And don't make the mistake of trying to yank a snagged hook or lure off bottom with the rod, or you'll snap it in two. If hooked up, jerk the line, not the pole.

Ultralight spinning tackle — 5-ounce reels and 4-foot rods — are sweet outfits for flipping tiny lures in the direction of panfish and trout. But it's neither clever nor fun to expect these minis to be an all-purpose spinning rig. Spinning is not the end-all, but does take top marks as a means of fool-proof, foul-proof fishing fun.

Chapter 5

Spin-Casting

The spin-cast reel followed on the heels of the open-face models, incorporating the same basic principles under a new guise.

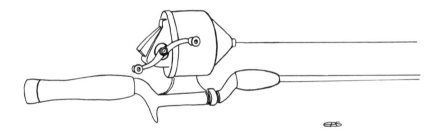

Instead of the spool being exposed, it's enclosed by a coneshaped cover. As the line peels off the spool, it threads onward through a hole in the housing.

Casting distance is not as impressive as with the open-face units, due in part to this added friction. Nor have the spin-cast reel spools the same large line capacity of conventional types. Most are brimfull with 100 yards of 8-pound test.

Many makers supply the line with the reel, but it's often wiry, heavy and of poor quality. Such monofilament should be discarded without even a wetting. Little dexterity is needed to cast a closed-face reel. They are operated by a pushbutton at the rear, which is compressed while casting until the moment of release. The line is free to run out once this pressure, which has snubbed it inside the housing, is removed.

Spin-casting is super-accurate, and an expert will consistently drop his lure on the bullseye. The cast can be controlled in flight with the push-button. A touch by the thumb arrests the lure in mid-air, which is very useful if it appears to be overshooting the target. To retrieve, turn the handle, which pops up a pin inside the housing. This pin picks up and places the line back on the spool while it rotates in conjunction with the cranking.

The location of the slipping-clutch control varies with makers. Some manufacturers incorporate it into a ring circling the housing, with others it's in the form of a dial on the body of the reel, while sometimes it's a star-shaped mechanism on the crank. Some indicate "pounds pressure" on a dial, but these are unreliable and should be ignored. Always test the clutch prior to your day's fishing, employing the same method as with open-face reels.

Line becoming fouled inside the housing is a fairly common ailment of these reels, since twists remain hidden when the spool is "under wraps."

Spin-casting really comes into its own for night fishing, there being no slack loops of line left dangling. Monofilament is the line for the spin-casting tribe, the braided variety's balky and totally unsatisfactory. Although a few closed-face reels are mounted on the underside of a straight handled rod as are open-face jobs, the majority of push-button models rest on top of a spincast rod in an off-set handle.

Baitcasting and spin-casting rods are similar in appearance, spincast foils being longer with the guides graduating in size. The average rod is 5½ -6 feet and constructed of hollow glass. Rod/reel combinations are often sold as a package, especially in the lower price ranges. Many of these inexpensive outfits are okay for casual anglers or tough-on-tackle kids. It's not only ease of casting which makes both brands of spinning tackle a joy to use, but the wide range and weights of the far-flung lures speak favorably for spinning's versatility.

Whenever possible — especially when alongside others — use the overhead cast. Timing must be slightly more critical than with the sidearm toss, but it's better from the standpoint of accuracy and safety. A "sidewinder" can be more dangerous than the venomous snake by the same name.

When circumstances dictate, the expert spin fisherman can hit the mark using a pot pourri of casting techniques. Underhand, overhead, sidearm, and even bow and arrow styles should be in his repertoire. With the latter, take extra care to ensure the hooks are grasped below the barbs. It's a good gimmick to have up your sleeve when a jungle of branches or brush precludes other methods.

Even flies can be fished with spinning tackle, by employing a clear float or "bubble" with a removable plug or a twist opening to allow water in as needed weight. Tie it on the end of the line and precede with a "dropper" several feet ahead to which a wet fly is attached. When casting drys, reverse the order.

This somewhat "crude" adaptation of an ancient art is seldom the route to comradeship with the fly-fishing purists, but it does work and can fill the creel. If you can tolerate the heavy drag when retrieving, there's no need to discard your casting lures. Some tried and true oldtime favorites are just as deadly on monofilament as they were on heavy braided lines.

However, their heft makes it necessary to lob them with a sidearm or underhand motion. The snap of an overhead cast will often result in a parting of the ways for line and lure. The average spinning enticement weighs ¼-ounce, but ultralight lures might go down to 1/16-ounce. Most range from ⅛ to ⅜ ounces.

Plenty of largemouth buffs lean toward heavier, noisier bait-casting topwater lures, even when pursuing them with spinning tackle. As with heavy lures, natural bait must be lofted forth gingerly. Spinning is unsurpassed for fishing live bait. On the end of limp and weightless monofilament, a worm will wriggle, a minnow swim, and a crayfish get into reverse gear. A tiny frog will kick freely along the surface until it disappears into a set of gaping jaws.

There's a definite niche for spin-casting, and an outfit belongs in the lineup of even the most skilled and adroit angler.

Chapter 6

Trolling

A knot of fishermen disdain trolling. These "activists" label it boring, dull, unsporting and a lazyman's sport. Hogwash! Trolling is what you make it. No one denys it's pleasantly relaxing — and why should they? A chance to unwind is becoming as rare as the dodo bird in today's rat race.

But it can also be laced with exciting anticipation. The angler who looks ahead is convinced he'll have a hefty strike when he swings past the next point, weedbed, or over an approaching shoal. Though some consider trolling unimaginative, it's ironic that those possessing imagination derive the greatest pleasure from it.

Another path to pleasure is to place a sonar Fish Lo-K-Tor where you can keep an eye on it. It's especially helpful when seeking lake trout and other deep-water species. Shoals, wrecks, boulders and fish all blink their presence on the device, instilling a new perspective into the game.

Trolling has been defined as the pulling or drawing of a lure behind a moving boat. It's doubtful that that author was an ardent angler, to have phrased it in such a mundane manner.

Trolling is not limited to tackle designed for the purpose. It can be successful with bait-casting and spinning gear; and there are old-timers who still stick with handlines. Trolling's the route to big fish in warm weather when they retreat to the depths. It's also productive for many big-game species like chinook, muskies and lake trout.

There's a wide range of superb trolling reels from which to choose, and most of the domestically manufactured models boast gear and clutch systems of superior quality to many imported brands. None of the freshwater fishes dictate the use of saltwater reels, so freshwater tackle is accordingly scaled down in size, weight and price. Star-drag and free-spool features are "musts". Some have a level-wind, but it's not essential or always practical.

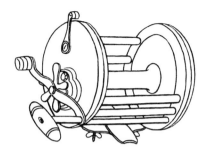

Trolling, like surf-casting, calls for conditioning. To outfight an angry, unsubmissive heavyweight one needs reserves of strength and stamina. When one thinks of trolling line, it's often in terms of metal — either copper or monel (a nickel alloy).

Only those not in the know will knock metal line fishing. The non-stretch wire lets you feel every strike or bottom bump, so it's a very sensibly sensitive way to fish. Kinking is a real danger with monel, so exercise caution when playing line out. Over-running can be prevented by thumb pressure on the lip of the spool.

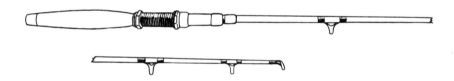

Some lines are marked at 50 and 100 feet intervals. Unless this has been done by the manufacturer, the fisherman is well advised to do so with tape, paint or nail varnish. A fine monel can be used on fly reels by spring anglers chasing lakers and brook trout near the surface, following ice-out. Braided nylon with a lead core inside half its length also gets the lure down to where the lunkers lurk.

But trolling isn't confined to the depths. Muskies, walleyes, pike and other relatively shallow-water species are hunted in this fashion. When shallow trolling, braided nylon, dacron or monofilament are all okay. The type of rod usually depends upon the quarry. Lake trouters lean toward a short, stiff staff, whereas the muskellunge angler looks for one that's longer and more limber.

A 5-foot rod boasting a hefty butt section can fill the bill for both. It should be dressed with top-quality guides and a roller top (especially essential for wire line).

The common technique when bringing a bruiser to net is to "pump" them in — lifting the pole and quickly winding in the line gained. Check a reel's gear ratio before purchasing. Winding in fish or weeds, or whatever, can be a tiring task. Most rods are outfitted with a rubber butt-cap, to be rammed into your "corporation" while battling a big one.

Trolling offers an opportunity to use giant-size plugs, spoons and spinners which are either too large for casting, or too heavy to retrieve comfortably. It's common knowledge that big bait takes big fish, and it's proven by the many tackle-busters taken annually on oversize baits, and on minnows or spoons dragged behind flashers or gang trolls (called cow bells or Christmas trees in certain regions).

You'll never convince the successful musky buff whose monstrous trophies took his 12-18 inch offerings that he would have done as well by casting tiny tidbits.

Trolling tackle should include a long, stout leader. As a chain is as strong as its weakest link, so is a trolling rig, as those who have had a swivel or lead break will sadly verify. A strong nylon leader allows a lure to give a natural performance. The place for a length of tough monofilament is between the line and metal leader.

This mode of angling is a logical technique in unfamiliar waters. Once the fish have been found, the fisherman can drop anchor and switch to casting. Trolling's not tedious, and is only as dull as the participant.

Chapter 7

Fly-Fishing

The fraternity of fly-fishers is no longer the exclusive, often aloof angling hierarchy of yesteryear. Died-in-the-wool purists are nearly trampled under in a stampede of newcomers. Most have evolved from spinning, which honed their enthusiasm to a keenness for new challenges.

And the landslide of green recruits is discovering the mystique woven around fly-fishing has needlessly kept them at bay. They wish they had discovered this fascinating and relatively uncomplicated form of fishing ages ago. New enthusiasts cannot quickly adapt. Fly-fishing is a science with countless facets, only one of which is casting the fly.

When casting, it's the line which carries the fly toward its destination, in contrast to the lure pulling the line as in baitcasting and spinning. Although a quality fly line is expensive, it's an important long-term investment.

Level lines are the most economic, but don't match the distance or presentation of double-taper types. In addition to the aforementioned, there are weight-forward lines plus floaters and sinkers. The latter are best when angling nymphs and wet flies. The serious fly fisher will own several lines, but happily doesn't need an equal number of reels. Extra spools are the answer unless his repertoire runs the gamut from salmon to sunfish.

An important point to keep in mind is the use of line best-suited to your rod. Knowledgeable tackle salesmen will steer you in the right direction. Most rods have the suited line size imprinted on the butt, or include the information in accompanying literature. Most devotees boast a battery of rods of varying lengths, weights and actions.

For starters, an all-round freshwater wand is an 8-8½ foot supple 4-5 ouncer. Slow to medium action is preferred. When tangling with salmon, a two-handed 9-9½ foot rod is the logical choice. At the other end of the spectrum, if stream fishing or pursuing panfish, an ultralight 5-6 footer can lay out a fly with a degree of delicacy which consistently pays off, even in heavily-pounded waters.

There are grizzled veterans who view all fly rods, except finely-crafted split bamboo, with disdain. Utter nonsense. A bamboo wand built by a master-craftsman is a beautiful work of art, but many of today's fiberglass models don't take a back seat action-wise, plus being lighter and tougher.

There is an immense satisfaction derived by presenting a fly naturally with a successful end result. There's an additional thrill from playing a finny quarry by hand, really getting the "feel" of the fight. A light leader is the equalizer, and by using a fine tippet the sportsman gives up the advantage of his virtually unbreakable line.

The tinier the fly the finer the tippet. The range in leader lengths is 7-12 feet. They can be hand-tied in graduating tests, which many anglers prefer. However, the commercial knotless type is tough to top from the standpoint of convenience and quality. Don't confuse fly leader material with spinning line. The monofilament made for leaders is much stiffer.

The final cog in the fly-fisher's machinery is the reel. Since the game is played by hand, it's the least important. If economizing during a confrontation with the initial outlay, here's where to do it. It's basically just a holder for the line.

 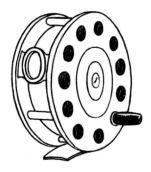

Single-action reels (rendering a turn per wind) are most popular. Multiplying reels' more rapid recovery is about double. And there are spring-wound automatics, which can quickly zip in yards of slack. Only tiny fish should be played with the reel — the others by hand. Hunting huskier species, such as salmon, calls for a large-capacity reel with 150 yards of backing as well as an adjustable drag.

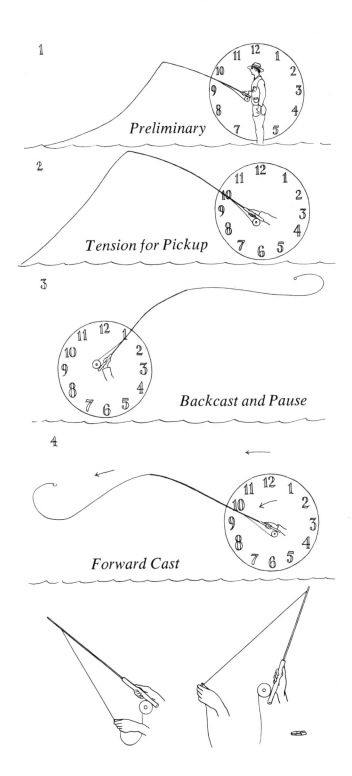

1   *Preliminary*

2   *Tension for Pickup*

3   *Backcast and Pause*

4   *Forward Cast*

31

Fly-casting cannot easily be described in words. The line should be picked up quickly and the backcast kept high. After the rod drives the line forward, and the loop unrolls to its full length, lift slightly so leader and fly uncoil ahead of the line. Timing is the important factor, so don't go at it too hard. Let the rod and line do the work.

To the predictable horror of so-called purists, we recommend strip-casting with natural bait such as worms and minnows. Pull the line from the reel and hand-hold. It will be carried through the guides by a forward flip of the rod.

This also works by letting the bait rest behind you and making an overhead cast, which will take your hand-held slack with it. Hordes of rainbow anglers are swinging to a fly-outfit outfitted with monofilament line. The long rod gives some control over the fish and the mono allows the worm or egg-sack to roll naturally along the bottom.

Conventional offerings are wet flies (tied to resemble dead insects), dry flies (imitating the live variety), and nymphs (duplications of larvae). There are also streamers, which "swim" minnow-like, and a wide range of bass bugs. Some of these are poppers, which noisily attract, others fake stranded moths, and there are the frog and mouse look-alikes.

For drys to float, they must be waterproofed, with silicone dressing usually getting the nod. False casting dries the fly and will add distance if desired. Although most merely fish the waters, stalking trout by casting to the rise is exciting and productive.

The ability to "match the hatch" or duplicate the existing insect population with the appropriate fly, can be a lifelong pursuit. Devoted fly fishermen become amateur entomologists (students of insect life).

A fly-fisherman's bailiwick is a beautiful one — placid pools where the duns dance, laughing brooks gurgling over white pebbles through fern-carpeted glades, and silvery moonlit lakes whose shadowed shores promise brawny bigmouth bass.

Chapter 8

There's Hot Action
Out In The Cold

Winter needn't be a period of relative inactivity for northern anglers. There are certain "chores" to be attended to, such as varnishing rods, greasing reels, rewinding guides, polishing lures and planning spring excursions, not to mention checking off the days until break-up.

A few fishing sorties will shorten the dragging months between freeze-up and ice-out, and are great therapy for withdrawal symptoms. Although lacking the action of their open water counterparts, deep-freeze outings are pleasant and sometimes exciting. Sunshine is the only known cure for those who get firmly hooked and deeply infected by the ice-fishing malady. Griping golf widows don't realize they're well off. How about those long-suffering wives whose hubbies close the shanty door behind them and take a lengthy sabbatical from today's pace and pandemonium?

Nearly all huts are home-made from plywood, and measure about 4 x 6 feet. Some are smaller, and a few are many times that size. There are some inventive portable units manufactured. These include rigid units on runners, pre-fabs which dismantle into banana-shaped sections which stack for easy towing, and even slick pop-up tents on sleds. All are a far-cry from the animal robes under which Indians and pioneer fishermen huddled.

A simple plastic or canvas windbreak will offer some protection from the north wind's blasts. Most permanent huts are heated by a coal, oil or propane stove, and the portables are generally warmed by a catalytic heater. The ice-angler has both a moral and legal responsibility to remove his winter quarters before break-up. Abandoning the shanty contributes to pollution, is a boating hazard when afloat, and distintegrates into unslightly debris littering the shorelines. Always mark the hole the hut sat over with a branch or stick, to warn others of the potential hazard.

In the final weeks of the winter season, angling in the sunlight under a roof of blue is a warm and welcome change from the usual cramped quarters. Shanty towns are sprinkled over the frozen surfaces of many of North America's more productive lakes. Many huts are for hire at $5-$10 per person, inclusive of transportation, fuel, bait and tackle. Ice fishing gear is inexpensive and uncomplicated. Begin with a cutting tool in the form of a "spud", saw or auger.

The "spud", or chisel, is the most common. Many sportsmen fashion their own by welding the steel blade to a metal handle or affixing it to the end of a stout hardwood pole. Chain saws will work, providing they're outfitted with an ice blade. These can be fashioned from wood-cutting teeth, with the help of a file, plus patience. Some manual augers will now bore through two or three feet of ice with ease. The resulting circular opening is large enough to accommodate the average catch. The motorized version of the above tool is the ultimate, but most prospects cop out when they spot the price tag.

After the hole has been opened, the floating chips of ice should be removed with a sieve or a "skimmer". Some devotees favor a short jigging rod, but most use a handline and tip-up or tilt. The former is a thin, flat piece of wood around which the line is wound. Unless hand-held, it's cradled in a holder fastened onto the floor or wall of the hut, or spiked into the ice beside the hole.

When a fish bites, the delicately-balanced stick dips down with most species. With bottom-feeders, such as whitefish, it bobs upwards. Spooled tilts are also popular. Many of these have a flag attached, which springs erect to signal a bite.

Monofilament line is favored by most anglers. The average testing strength is 10-pounds, with pike and trout fishermen leaning toward stronger lines. Braided line, being prone to freezing, is not as well suited. A great choice is fly line, with the addition of a monofilament leader. It's strong, seldom tangles, resists freezing and will endure indefinitely. The thickness of this line guarantees ease of handling when playing a fish.

Spoons with a weighted nose — which come in a wide range of sizes — are very effective, and imitate a feeding minnow when correctly jigged. The weighted fly is also tops in some locales. Some plugs and spoons "swim" in circles when raised or lowered. A favorite is a life-like fish carved by Ontario Indians. Although now outfitted with hooks, it's nearly identical to the decoy used centuries ago to lure trout under the tynes of a spear which the Indian kept poised over the hole.

The majority of ice fishing is a wait-and-watch game, live or natural bait providing the enticement. Bait fish are first choice, with worms, larvae, maggots, frozen smelt, salted minnows, cut-bait, fish eyes, and other imaginative tidbits being productive.

Two and three hook spreaders are widely used when bottom fishing. They consist of a central sinker with an embedded swivel to which the line is attached. Like spider's legs, wires protrude from the weight, to which snelled hooks are affixed. You'll need a needle-sharp gaff if you hope to elevate a bruiser to your level.

If fishing the same hole on a regular basis, it pays dividends to chum the bottom. Pre-baiting can be with salted minnows, tapioca, barley and other grains. Fish are inclined to frequent a spot where a free handout awaits. Beware of over-baiting, which can "sour" the bottom.

Don't venture on unfamiliar ice-covered waters before cautiously checking your route. Currents and underwater springs account for channels and pockets of dangerously thin ice. One person requires two inches of clear blue ice, three inches is the minimum for a group in single file, and it takes 7½ inches for small vehicles.

Electronic sonar devices, such as the Lowrance Fish Lo-K-Tor, will read depth, underwater terrain and even the presence of fish before you commence to drill, chop, or cut. With the assistance of anti-freeze simply create a puddle of water and place the face of the transducer in it. It will pass along this information right through the ice. In deep-freeze fishing, an ounce of know-how is worth pounds of fish.

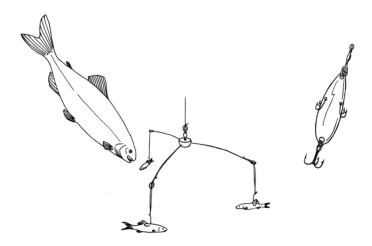

Chapter 9

Tackle Tips

The success or failure of an angling outing is often determined by the degree of foresight in preparing for the junket. Learning by experience is a life-long lesson, and there are countless hints and tips which will swell catches and enjoyment.

Even the largest tackle box on the dealer's shelf isn't commodious enough for all the clobber which accompanies some anglers on their excursions. Even when being initiated, you're well-advised to purchase a titanic tackle-toter. It will soon be chock-full. Cork-lined compartments will keep hook rusting minimal by absorbing the moisture off damp lures.

Good quality fiberglass and plastic boxes are more durable than easily-dented aluminium jobs, as well as being impervious to the rust which consumes steel models. Pocket-boxes are handy when stream fishing. So are today's fly boxes, which boast unique improvements over the old books and pouches.

Tackle boxes have a habit of opening and dumping their treasures during transit, in spite of snaps and catches. They must be tough to withstand the punishment railroads and airlines mercilessly inflict upon baggage.

Snub a webbed belt tightly around the box when shipping by air or rail. Locking doesn't make much sense. A thief will likely walk off with the entire kit 'n' caboodle. And it's difficult for the average vague fishing-type to keep track of a key.

Rods should always be shipped in stout cases or tubes, which will withstand those bruising beatings. Theft or loss could spell ruination of a trip, so carry insurance in the form of an extra reel and pack-rod inside your suitcase. No angler should ever venture far from home without a back-up outfit. Carry a stock of treble hooks and split rings in various sizes. Rusty or broken barbs and weakend rings should be replaced pronto.

It's amazing how many striking fish stay hooked when the barbs are needle-sharp. Touch them up periodically with a hook-hone. A flexible, razor-thin filleting knife does a quick cleaning job, but requires frequent sharpening. An oil-stone in the kit will prove invaluable.

Lures should be chosen with an eye to quality, not price. Spoons with baked-on enamel look more attractive under water, and have a more lengthy life-span than do the hastily-sprayed lures. The same

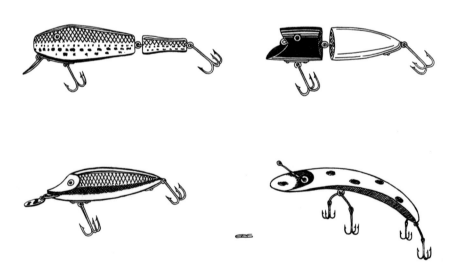

Bait Casting Plugs

guidelines apply to metallic finishes. For some subtle reason, nickel-plating takes more fish than does chrome. Seldom do cheap imitations of famous lures produce as well as the originals. Most are price propositions, with the subsequent sacrifice in quality.

A complete lure assortment should include wobbling and darting spoons in several sizes; top-water, shallow and deep-running plugs; a wide range of spinners; plus jigs, plastic worms and sundry other geegaws.

Leaders should be used only when fishing those species boasting a mouthful of shearing fangs. A lure tied directly to the line gives a better performance than does one hampered by a stiff leader.

Pennies are still all that separate a strongly constructed leader from a hastily-assembled poor second choice. Nylon-coated wire is tops, but carefully check both snap and swivel. The swivel must be free and fool-proof, and the snap should be hooked at the end so it cannot pull loose. Heavier sinkers than necessary lessen chances of success by hampering the action of the lure or bait.

Deep-trolling, swift currents, heavy tides, or big baitfish are the only circumstances which dictate the use of hefty sinkers. Never use more weight than is necessary. Split shot and lead wire are what most experts prefer.

Snelled hooks are a needless extravagance for all but bait-casters. Tie a short-shank single hook directly to the monofilament line, bearing in mind a tiny barb will grip as tenaciously as a meat hook. Empty film cans are great containers for split-shot, loose hooks, snap swivels, and other odds and ends.

When tying on leaders, hooks and lures, always give the knot a double-checking tug to ensure it's securely tied.

A bobber has its place, such as when suspending live bait above a heavy weedbed or drifting it over rocks and snags. Stock several sizes, using the smallest which fills the particular bill. By using quill and pencil floats, which offer less resistance to biting fish than do the round types, a wary quarry is less likely to spit out the bait.

Your tackle box or fishing vest should contain a reel-repair kit. Oil and grease are both important, as is a tiny screwdriver, suitable wrench and pliers. A pictorial x-ray of the reel is useful for those unfamiliar with its innards.

Screws, handle, bail springs and tension cap are the parts most likely to need replacing. On-the-spot rod repairs are often possible — dependent on the nature of the break. A couple of spare ferrules are worthwhile, and a stick of instant-drying ferrule cement is an essential. Ferrules can be removed by a steady pull, coupled with heat applied to the glued portion.

A metal pin — such as a nail — inserted in a broken top section which is then splinted and wound with plastic tape, will usually hold the rod together temporarily. The only guide that's really essential is the top. Always carry two extras, one the same size and the other a size larger. If guide windings begin to unravel, the thread can be lacquered down with an application of clear nail polish.

Tenacious gas and oil odors, and even human scent on lures or bait can be responsible for a skunking. Fishermen in the know, carry a tube or bar of soap to scrub hands and lures frequently. Matches in a waterproof container or coated with wax should occupy a compartment in your box. An everlasting, indestructable "metal match" might be a life-saver some day.

Another useful item is a small, waterproof flashlight — with batteries reversed until needed. It can serve as a signal light in the event of trouble, or as a running light if overtaken by darkness. The wading gang should have a patching kit handy, plus a chunk of old innertube to mend large tears. If waters are swift, a wading staff is needed. It acts as a third leg, providing the stability of a tripod. A ski pole works well in lieu of the real McCoy.

Foul-weather fishermen can eliminate the annoyance and frustrations of iced guides by coating the inside with vaseline. It's tough to handle an open-face reel while wearing gloves, so a hand-warmer will restore life to numb fingers between casts. These are but a handful of tips, most learned the hard way. Hopefully, they'll save you from some of that grief.

Chapter 10

Live Bait - Naturally

Certain anglers decry or scorn the use of live bait, harboring a cockeyed notion that fishing naturally is unsporting. Nuts. In fact, fishing natural bait is a science calling for as much knowledge and expertise as does the wafting of a No. 14 dry fly to a delicate landing on a crystal trout pool.

It's not the bait, but the tackle, which spells sport. Versatility pays off, and the all-round angler will fish flies, lures or live bait — whichever is dedicated by the particular situation. The fact that worms have provided the last meal for more fish than any other bait or lure is indisputable.

Most popular are nightcrawlers, also known as dew-worms. Both names signify that they emerge from the ground after dark, when the grass is damp with dew, or after a watering or shower. When "worm picking" tread softly and probe with a subdued light. Sneakers and a head-lamp are made-to-order. To get a sure grip on these slippery customers and avoid injuring them, strap a tin of sawdust or sand to your leg, and periodically dip your slimey fingers into the can.

There are more sophisticated worming devices than a deft hand, but beware their dangerous undercurrents. One consists of two metal rods which are jammed into the ground at one end and connected to an extension cord at the other. The electricity is not only shocking to worms, but has been responsible for some human electrocutions.

Heat is the prime crawler killer. In hot weather don't store them in your car trunk during transit. Too often a sportsman is left gasping and gagging on lifting the lid off the worm box. The referigerator is the spot for them in the home. Ensure the container top is snugly secured, or the little woman will be greeted by these exploratory creatures festooned from every shelf, bowl, and bottle. Hardly the way to win over the "opposition."

Black peat is best for keeping bait lively. You'll have the same brand of fishing if "garden hackles" are kept cool and moist, and housed in this fodder. They won't wiggle and squirm as much in sphagnum moss — although it's a lot cleaner and more widely used. The smaller "garden variety" angleworms and redworms are often preferred for stream trout and panfish.

There's an art to worm fishing, based on a natural presentation. Hook the crawler once through the collar with a fine barb, as little weight as possible and no leader to impede its enticing action. In turbulent and cloudy waters they're extremely deadly, and are a winning ticket to taking trout in cold weather when they lie dormant near the bottom.

Minnows rank No. 2 in popularity with live bait fishers. Keeping baitfish in fine fettle is another kettle of fish. The water should be aerated and supplemented by a constant cool flow. Many bait dealers sell them in oxygen-filled plastic bags in an inch or two of water. They'll survive in these for days, unless overheated or overcrowded.

Avoid "putting your eggs in one basket" by carrying bait in a couple of bags. Catching minnows on location is preferred. This can be done with a trap, umbrella net or seine. Be sure to check regulations first. Bait the trap with oatmeal balls, and the same cereal will lure them over the net.

Many bodies of water have been "ruined" by the introduction of coarse or diseased fish through thoughtless dumping of surplus bait-fish into the lake at day's end. Do this over the home garbage can, garden, or toilet bowl.

Although most fishermen have a preference for live minnows, dead baitfish produce very well at times. When casting or trolling minnows, a good method is to thread them to the hook by pulling the line under the skin with a baiting needle. If still-fishing, hook them just ahead of the dorsal fin, through both lips, or the eyes.

You'll get more action from the bait by slicing off a portion of its tail. Their subsequent vigorous action makes them more enticing to gamefish.

Frogs are excellent bass bait, and are recommended for certain other species too. Although a hook through the leg permits them to swim more effortlessly, it's folly when angling among heavy vegetation and snags.

Most fish take their food head-first, so by the time the quarry has stopped running and you've set the hook, the line can be hopelessly entangled. Under such circumstances, the fisherman should imbed his barb through the frog's lips. He can then lean into the rod almost at once.

If fish are skulking under banks, rocks and other under-water lairs, it's necessary to weight the line. A couple of split shot will usually suffice.

Frogs will keep between outings in moss and water at basement temperatures. They can also be kept in damp moss in the refrigerator, where they become dormant and enter a state of semi-hibernation.

Anyone who has fished smallmouth bass with crayfish will readily testify they're murder on bronzebacks. They're the trick with many other fish, especially if crayfish are native to the waters. Many anglers favor removing the claws, so they're less likely to crawl under rocks with tackle in tow. Crayfish are best hooked through the tail. Store them as you would frogs. Leeches are likely the most durable bait available, short of metals and plastics. As well as being long-lasting, they can prove effective.

They can be gathered by tossing a tied chunk of fresh meat into their habitat, hauling it back several hours later. You'll usually have reaped enough "bloodsuckers" for days of fishing.

Hellgrammites — the Dobson fly larvae — are hot for trout and bass. They can best be harvested by stretching a screen across the flow and overturning stones upstream. The dislodged hellgrammites will be swept onto the mesh by the current. Hook them through the collar, avoiding their princers which can render a nasty nip.

Shrimp are widely used in the south, creek fishermen favor grasshoppers or crickets, and musky anglers have been known to use mice. As a matter of fact, the woods and waters are literally crawling with bait for the angler with versatility and imagination.

Most productive for steelhead are trout or salmon eggs. They're usually tied to maline or nylon bags about the size of a dime. West coast experts are skilled in the preparation of roe and have several favorite techniques. One is to wrap fresh eggs in paper towelling and drain in the refrigerator overnight. The skein is then cut into chunks and each piece coated with borax by shaking it in a bag of the powder. The roe is then placed in glass jars, topping with more borax. Refrigerated, it will keep for weeks without freezing.

Milk eggs are another winner. The split skeins are allowed to drain for several hours and then sprinkled lightly with Sodium Sulfite, Merk No. 5201. The eggs are wrapped in towelling, and frozen in plastic bags. "Spawn bags" should bounce along the bottom freely by using as little lead as necessary. A short-shank No. 2, No. 4, or No. 6 hook gets the nod from most.

When presenting natural bait, do it naturally. Shun leaders, heavy weights, and a bobber, unless it's a must. If those who scorn live bait fishing were more flexible, they'd find their rods bending more frequently too.

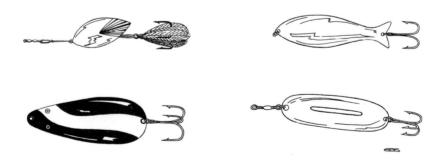

Trolling and Bait-Casting Spoons

Chapter 11

Landing And Handling

"The one that got away" tales of woe are legion. Many a potential prize eludes capture due to the angler's eleventh-hour ineptness.

Glance over any congregation of anglers and you'll note numbers are netless. Presumably, this group is comprised of optimists with utmost confidence in their hand-landing techniques, and pessimists who don't anticipate the need for a net. Nets are myriad in shape and size. A smallfish model with a shallow bag and short handle usually meets the requirements of the stream fisherman.

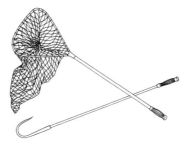

The elastic loop on the handle can be slung over the shoulder, or snapped onto the back of a fishing vest. In theory, it's readily available, yet nearly snag-proof. However, any angler who's had the mesh caught in brush, the elastic stretched taut then catapult onto his skull might beg to differ. Once walloped, twice shy. Thus, the practical folding net with the band steel frame fitting into a handy belt pouch has won a following. It's perfect for working along brush-girdled banks and cannot get hung-up.

Nets should be scaled to your ambitions and potential prey. A long-handled model is a requisite when boat fishing, and musky hunters usually sally forth with a stout four-foot deep twine bag hooped onto a strong 5-6 foot handle.

Many tyros and even slow-to-learn veterans persist in scooping their catch tail-first. Such foolishness has cost many a lunker. Fish aren't equipped with a reverse gear, so always take them head-first. Their thrashing only drives them deeper into the imprisoning confines of the net.

Check the strength of the net regularly, and further inspect it for wear and tear. Nylon is grand, being waterproof and almost indestructible. Cotton mesh rots and requires frequent replacing. Make sure when you finally catch up to that "one for the wall" it doesn't enter the front door and leave by the back.

A gaff in the strong grip of an expert is an effective tool for latching onto and swinging lunkers over the gunwales. A gaff is a large hook, solidly set in a handle from which it curves away for sure, quick penetration. It's usually barbless and should always be kept needle-sharp. A green gaffer is well advised to serve his apprenticeship getting the swing of it with his own catches.

Ice fishermen, being restricted by the confines of their minute patch of open water, have discovered a huge treble hook is a good substitute for a single barb. A gaff should serve as an auxiliary landing device. Its puncture is mostly fatal, so "returnables" should be netted or otherwise boated unharmed.

Some Atlantic salmon experts use a "tailer"; a wire noose. This is slipped over the tail and drawn tight around the salmon's slim caudal peduncle. By hoisting the tail out of the water, the salmon is rendered helpless.

A sharp rap between the eyes will pacify most bruisers, and some anglers tote a billy for this purpose. If the fish is still in the water when whacked, aim accurately or wave goodbye. It's sensible to save this coup de grâce for subduing a fighter after it's boated.

A few anglers possess the expertise to scorn all landing devices except the one they were born with. Hand-landing is quick and sure. When a fish's gills are firmly compressed by thumb and fingers, it becomes inert and can be flipped aboard with ease.

Some buffs land their bass by grasping the lower jaw with thumb and forefinger. It's effective, providing you have an openjawed, played-out largemouth, and the lure or hook is out of harm's way.

Top marks go to the Atlantic salmon fraternity who sub an iron grip for a tailer to dispatch their quarry. Digging a thumb and forefinger deeply into a fish's eye-sockets will make them immobile, but it's not as positive as the gill-compressing technique. Furthermore, it can cause eventual cataracts or immediate blindness, so should not be practiced on fish destined for release.

Squeezing a fish tightly while removing the hook could result in permanent internal damage. If a fish has "swallowed" the hook, cut the line and let it go. Its gastric juices will eventually dissolve the metal. Plated hooks resist this deterioration, and fishermen who "give a damn" should boycott those barbs.

If you wish to release a played-out fish or one suffering from the "bends", move it gently back and forth under water until this form of artificial respiration brings it around and it's able to depart under its own steam. A pike-gag is an inexpensive, effective device for keeping their jaws agape while removing the hooks. A disgorger and long-nosed pliers should always be handy.

Your catch will be firm and flavorsome if killed and cleaned immediately. If there are no cooling facilities on hand, keep them alive until it's time to wind in and head homeward. Most don't live long on a stringer, but if this is the holding device, remember to lift it aboard when the boat is moving swiftly. Impaling the catch through both lips forestalls drowning.

A wire-mesh corral, such as many cottagers have built at their shore, is a great idea. For the angler on the move, the collapsible fish-keeper (a mini-corral) does a good job. The disadvantage is when moving from place to place, when it must be pulled in. A plus for this device is the fact that small fish taken earlier in the day can be exchanged for their larger brethern, should they start biting.

Trout containers vary from the net type, which zips onto the bottom of a fishing vest, to many styles of creels. The rubber-lined shoulder bags are poor — especially in hot weather. Fish heap on top of one another, and in hot weather soon spoil within the oven-like confines.

The felt-covered bags are great, providing they're kept wet so the interior is cooled via the evaporation principle. It's tough to top the venerable willow creel, with its roomy interior and adequate ventilation. Split willow is the most durable. If a fish is worth keeping, it's worth keeping well.

Chapter 12

Pool To Platter

It's a shame — even a crime — to carelessly cause a gamefish to spoil. Following a valiant struggle, a noble adversary deserves a better fate. If an angler isn't prepared to take suitable steps to ensure his catch reaches the table, then he should release it unharmed.

But mountains of fish regularly degenerate because fishermen are too damn lazy to clean them, or ignore the basic rules for keeping them firm and fresh. An ice-chest is a practical, inexpensive container for the catch. Keep the fish on top of the ice, for if they slip down the sides into the melt-off they'll soon become mushy.

It's not as readily available as frozen water, but dry ice is a real boon to the fishing fraternity. It's astonishingly heavy, and a 10-inch block weighs some 50-pounds. That's more than needed, except on lengthy outings. A thin slab will keep fish frozen for days.

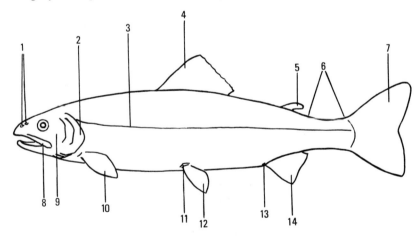

(1) nostrils	(6) caudal peduncle	(11) fleshy appendage
(2) gill cover	(7) caudal fin	(12) pelvic fin
(3) lateral line	(8) maxillary	(13) anus
(4) dorsal fin	(9) cheek	(14) anal fin
(5) adipose fin	(10) pectoral fin	

It "melts" into CO_2 vapor, not liquid. The spiggot of the cooler should be left open so that these gasses may escape. Handling it can be hazardous, and should be avoided if possible. The temperature of dry ice is minus 109 degrees, and direct contact results in an extremely painful burn.

When gutting a fish, simply slice the belly open and remove the innards, taking care to scrape away all traces of blood from along the backbone. If the head is left attached, cut out the gills as well.

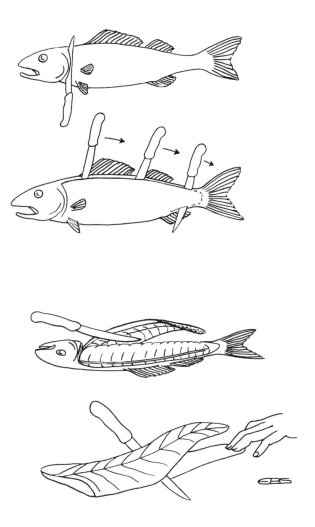

Special care is called for if the "catch of a lifetime" is slated for a permanent place of honor above the homefire. Slicing it along the belly will ruin it for mounting.

The best procedure is to freeze it intact, leaving cleaning and skinning for the taxidermist. If it's not possible, due to isolation or lack of freezing facilities, make a short cut directly under the rib cage along one side. Remove the innards through this slit, and cut out the gills very carefully. Wrap the taxidermist-bound lunker in a wet cloth, which will keep the skin and fins from drying out. Many an angler rues the day he opted to eat a trophy catch, reasoning he'd soon land a bigger one. That day seldom, if ever, arrives.

A mounted fish helps you to relive vividly those memorable moments time after time. Such pleasant recollections far outweigh the initial cash outlay for mounting.

Filleting is the favored method of cleaning the catch, and calls for a razor-sharp flexible blade. The first step is a deep cut from back to belly, just behind the head. Pare the meat from the bones by slicing downwards and backwards from head to tail. Keep the knife pressed firmly against the ribs as you cut. Flip the fish over, and repeat the performance.

To skin the two resulting slabs, lay them on a flat surface, skin down. Starting from the tail-end, press the blade under the flesh and against the skin. Pushing the knife forward on a slight angle cleanly separates skin from meat. Small fish are best scaled and gutted, whereas lunkers are often steaked.

An important rule to remember is clean a fish as soon as it's dead. The gastric juices are still active, and can quickly taint the meat. Also, if it's left exposed in hot weather, the blow flies will zero in on the carcass, which will be crawling with maggots within minutes. The larval fluke infestation, known as black spot, appears as small dark dots on many species. Skinning solves the problem.

Another common larva is the yellow grub, which bores into the flesh forming a cyst. These can be flicked out with the point of a knife. The fish lice which live on fins and gill covers are also harmless. When cleaning the catch, you'll frequently discover flat white tapeworms and string-like roundworms inside the body cavity. Fear not. Fish are no "wormier" than other creatures. A fish's parasites won't be the death of you, and are destroyed by cleaning and cooking.

Chapter 13

How Hip Are Hypotheses?

Every fisherman has his pet theories, all of which prove to be infallible — at some time or other.

Some are based on logic, embracing more fact than fiction. Many others, in spite of armies of believers, are pure and simple nonsense — old wives' tales perpetuated by generations of gullibles.

Most theories have been neither proved nor disproved, but to shake zealots loose from their adamant beliefs is akin to converting a religious fervent to another faith.

John Alden Knight's Solunar Theory has legions of followers. Pin-pointing on the clock the four daily feeding periods — two major and a couple of minor ones — results from a formula involving sun, moon and tides.

The predicted bursts of activity average about an hour in length, and the lists of times for the entire year are available in booklet form. This slim publication is a Bible to many fishermen, as well as those hunters subscribing to the solunar theory.

It is said to affect every living creature, man included. Some claim that cows tell them when to go fishing, their grazing habits being reportedly determined by the same schedule. That's when birds sing and squirrels scamper, so claim the devout disciples of J. A. Knight.

Fish are sensitive to atmospheric pressure changes, and a rising glass is an indication that angling will improve, whereas when it's sinking some refuse to budge from book and bottle.

Barometric pressures have a definite effect on fish and animal life, and a needle on the upswing coincides with a general buoying of human spirits. But it's no sure-fire formula you'd want to bet your Hardy rod on.

Rain sends the fair-weather fishermen scampering for shelter, but is no deterrent to the ardent. Some stream fishers even welcome a shower or downpour.

The run-off from the banks and down the swelled feeder streams carries an abundance of insect life with it, triggering trout into a feeding spree.

Also, muddy or cloudy waters dull the keen edge of their inherent wariness. The raindrops pocking the surface decrease the likelihood of the angler being spotted, plus the fact there's no fish-spooking shadow to be concerned over. Rain cools tepid waters and increases the oxygen content, which acts like a tonic.

According to many self-ordained soothsayers, you don't need a barometer or even a weather forecast to know when rain is on the way. Its approach is heralded by a ring around the moon, a haloed setting sun, a red dawn and even busily bathing birds.

However, if that rain is accompanied by a thunderstorm, it can be a different story, especially for the lake fisherman. Only a reckless fool stays on the lake in the midst of lightning. To be struck by a bolt from the black is not necessarily painful, but its rather final.

Subaqueous vibrations caused by a clap thunder may terminate fast action abruptly. The devastating effectiveness of these hellish peals from on high fluctuates in accordance with the nature of the lake's bottom and the strata below it.

The thermometer theory is not a whimsical one. Those with the patience to scout a body of water via thermometer will frequently reap rewards for their efforts.

One must first be clued in to the Fahrenheit temperature range preferred by each species. These are: brook trout 55°-65°, lake trout 45°-55°, brown trout 55°-70°, rainbow trout 60°-70°, walleye 55°-70°, maskinonge 60°-70°, pike 50°-70°, largemouth bass 68°-78°, and smallmouth bass 65°-70°.

During summer's steamy dog days, many fish go off their feed and pike are reputed to ignore the angler's temptations because they've lost their teeth and suffer from sore gums. True, feeding sprees are less frequent, but as for that gummy theory—hogwash! Their fangs aren't spewed en masse, but fall out and are replaced year 'round.

Dog days weather is usually a combination of extreme heat and prolonged periods of relative calm. With little surface turbulence, the water gets low in oxygen and the fish become sluggish. This is especially true in those lakes sparse on vegetation.

The concept that the best action occurs on cloudy days when there's a slight chop, is easily explained. Since fish can't close their eyes or dilate their pupils, they shun the discomfort of the sun's bright glare and seek shade, or submerge to the shadowy depths.

With the sun obscured by cloud and with the waves further diffusing the light, they feed near the top and in the shallows.

The theory that fishermen should speak in whispers for fear of frightening their quarry is illogical. Only extreme above-water noises are detrimental.

But a carelessly-heaved anchor, objects dropped in boats, and a heavy foot on the stream's bank will panic the prey.

"When the wind's from the east, the fish bite the least. When it blows from the west, fish bite the best". A catchy rhyme that's fairly factual, probably because an easterly blow is often synonymous with falling barometric pressures and stormy weather.

Many eye-appealing brightly colored lures are primarily designed to catch fishermen. But it's proven that certain colors are attractive to the fish. After conducting experiments, scientists listed yellow, red and blue as the top trio, in that order.

Fish are endowed with a keen sense of smell, as proven by the salmon's amazing return to the stream of his birth.

A spoon or spinner is sometimes made more effective by the addition of a minnow or fish tail impaled on the hooks. It's probably scent rather than sight which spells the difference.

Oil of aniseed is a favorite fish-coy, and some dip lures and live bait into this licorice-flavored concoction before tossing them out.

Ever notice how the guy operating the outboard motor has less luck than others in the boat? It's because he's handling his lures with hands which smell of gas and oil. It requires a lengthy submersion before that repulsive odor is washed off, during which time fish avoid his offering like the plague. Even our natural human scent when transferred to a bait will make fish shy away.

If you spot a bar of soap in an angler's tackle box, you can assume he's a fellow who knows the score. Scrub hands and lures thoroughly and often during the course of a day's fishing.

It's okay to theorize, but few creatures' habits are as unexplainable and as unpredictable as those of fish. But, after all, that's one reason fishing's fun. The best theory of all is to fish whenever and wherever you get the opportunity, irrespective of weather, water, whims, or whatever.

Chapter 14

Get Into The Swim

You'll catch more fish if you think like one. Some kindly refer to it as "reading the waters".

Notice how the "lucky" fisherman gives regular repeat performances. And his fine catches aren't necessarily confined to his own bailiwick. Even when he journeys to far-flung fisheries, he still pulls a hare from the hat. He comes home dragging those tails behind him not through luck, but know-how. He's undoubtedly a fishy-eyed fisherman. Even when viewing strange waters, his wealth of knowledge tells him where the quarry is lurking, and why.

To translate waters, terrain, weather and species intelligently into the formula for success is no mean achievement. It results from an in-depth study of fishes' habits and habitat. The angler must carry the keys for unlocking many submerged secrets. One is an awareness of the temperatures various species seek and prefer. To cite extremes, there's as much chance of hooking into a lake trout in 70 degree shallows as a largemouth bass in 50-foot depths.

By applying a wealth of information when fishing new waters, those time-tested pieces fit together until the puzzle becomes a clear picture. Drop-offs, shoals, rocky points and river mouths are all good bets in any lake. And if bass are your bag, you should look for the lily pads and stump-riddled bays. Largemouths have no fear of swimmers, and will often cruise along a busy beach feeding on the tasty treats they've unearthed.

It's an uncommon angle, but casting among them will often pay big dividends. A bathing beauty is a girl worth wading for and an old Mossback even more so.

Many cottage-girdled lakes aren't worth a darn in daytime due to the powerboat jockeys with skiers in tow who manage to keep it churned to a froth. But when these hot-rodders doff the silks at dusk, the fish come out of hiding. They do their foraging in the still of the night and the smart fishermen will do likewise.

Stream fishing is a tough assignment for the tyro. "Creep before you walk" advice is ignored by the novice who will likely tramp to the rim of many promising, but unproductive pools, until he discovers his heavy step and silhouette have spooked the quarry into their lairs. When he learns to creep stealthily to streamside he'll begin to fill his creel.

And he'll eventually find out that to flail those straight, still stretches of stream is an exercise in futility — time wasted on empty waters. Responding to their inherent wariness, most fish seek the protection offered by undercut banks, log jams, brush piles and overhanging trees.

When rivers run high and turbulant, trout look for a quiet resting place. They find current-splitting boulders ideal, with most offering an added bonus in the feed which passes by "left and right".

A narrows is another favorite of feeding fish. You'll also find them at the tail of a pool and in the oft-overlooked slick at the head of a rapids.

In beaver ponds trout seldom inhabit the deep, dark pool behind the dam. That's because it's usually silted, warm and void of vegetation. They generally congregate in the flooded-over original stream bed. In summer, fish, like folks, look for a respite from the heat. That's when you'll often find them gathered where the cool flows of feeder streams spill into the main waterway.

And the aerated shallow rapids, rich in oxygen, will also yield good catches of trout which seemingly appear from nowhere to sock your spinner or suck in your fly. During and after a rain the murky waters cloud their caution and spur them into a feeding spree.

If you scout your opponents and familiarize yourself with their tricks and tactics it will be a brand new ball game. And you'll be making your pitch with a crystal ball.

Chapter 15

Some Solutions To Knotty Problems

The price paid for carelessly and ineptly-tied knots is often steep. It's saddening and maddening to stare at tell-tale twists on the end of the line after a lunker has "snapped" loose.

The mystery of how it was able to escape unravels as easily as did the knot which joined line to lure. It's no cinch to become acquainted with the entire fishermens' repetoire of hitches, bends and splices. That list is longer than the legendary 'ones that got away'.

A guy who confused reef knots with grannies when he was a cub-scout shouldn't get too wrapped up in the subject. A solid knowledge of a varied handful will suffice for most freshwater angling. An illuminating magnifier pinned on your vest will be a big aid when working with fine monofilament. These gadgets are invaluable during nocturnal fishing and are a great crutch — day or night — for those not blessed with 20-20 eagle-eyesight.

The junctions illustrated in this chapter are a few proven favorites which, when correctly tied, will help keep "tight lines" taut.

TURLE KNOT — It's a time-tested way of attaching hooks, lures or flies to monofilament. After threading the nylon through the eye, make a slip knot and loop it over the hook.

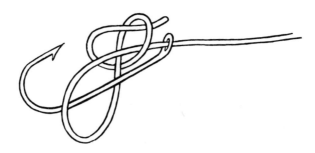

IMPROVED CLINCH KNOT — As the name suggests, it's a stronger version of its predecessor. Top-notch for attaching lures, hooks and swivels to spinning line, it's also an excellent way to join fly to tippet. After passing the line or leader through the eye, double it back against itself and give it several twists. Slide the end between eye and coils, through the loop, and slowly snub tight.

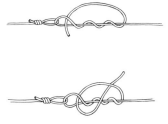

PALOMAR KNOT — It's quickly tied and retains 100 per cent line strength. After looping the line through the eye, bring the loop up and under the double line and tie a loose overhand knot. Holding the knot between thumb and forefinger of one hand, pull the loop over the hook with the other. Draw the knot to the top of the eye and tighten.

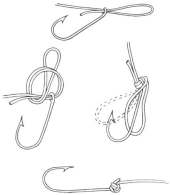

SINGLE WATERLOOP — This is also called the buffer knot and is mostly used for joining strands of different diameters. The ends are brought together and each is loop-tied over the other.

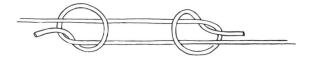

BLOOD KNOT — This is a simple, satisfactory way to join two lengths of line. Their ends are wrapped around each other half a dozen times and then brought back and tucked through the middle from opposite sides. The result is a strong, neat junction.

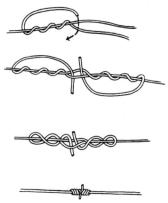

ALBRIGHT SPECIAL — It's primarily utilized with an extra-long leader, since this knot keeps casting fraction minimal. An important point to remember is always make a dozen or more wraps with the line before tightening by pulling on the line and the loose end of the leader.

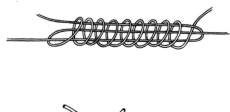

JAM HITCH — This is used to join the line to the leader loop, and many prefer it because it is easily untied. The end of the line is knotted, which jams securely when the main knot is tightened.

Chapter 16

Pests And Perils

The great outdoors harbors fewer dangers than those lurking in the concrete jungles, on traffic-clogged freeways and in the home.

These words are not intended to minimize the hazards which might be encountered when walking the woods or wading the waters. But "happiness is a fishing trip" only when it's not shrouded by "what if" worries and ultra-caution, which kill the spirit of adventure.

The proverbial ounce of prevention precludes most serious problems and should any occur, the majority can be coped with by common sense. Ever notice the happiest people take the longest strides, while worry-warts shuffle through life with their eyes on the ground?

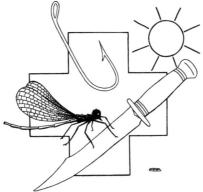

Biting, boring, blood-sucking insects sometimes threaten piscatorial pleasures. Black flies, mosquitoes and no-see-'ems can best be classed as annoyances. The correct clothing (as described elsewhere in this book) provides a partial deterrent. Headnets, though hot, confining, claustrophobic contraptions, are 100% effective in keeping bugs at bay. Many repellents are effective, with frequent applications required on hot days when they'll drip away with perspiration.

Chemicals in certain brands murder plastics and rubber, eating through tackle boxes, deteriorating lines and tainting lures. Non-smokers engage in more bug-battles than do cigar and pipe-puffers. Most insects — especially black flies — have a definite aversion to smoke.

Many seasoned outdoorsmen smugly return from the north woods unblemished, while others "in the same boat" have been virtually eaten alive. The reason may be Vitamin B1. Injected or taken in pill form, it makes one unappealing to the black fly. Consult with your doctor before getting this "prescription" filled.

Chiggers loathe most repellents, and a solution of baking soda will relieve their itching aftermath. Ticks are something else. These big, boring, repulsive creatures are best removed from the skin by touching their backsides with a lighted cigarette or match. If you attempt to whisk them way or yank them off, the infectious head might remain buried behind.

Bees, hornets and wasps occasionally are to be painfully reckoned with. Anyone who's been the object of wrath from an angry hive of yellowjackets will from there on in react like a gun-shy dog whenever he hears their buzzing.

Baking soda is a good antidote for stings by this terrible trio. Bees leave their stingers embedded, so pluck them out with tweezers. Snake bites can be serious, even fatal. The chance of encountering one of this continent's four venomous reptiles is extremely remote. The water mocassin and coral snake are confined to the southern U.S. with the copperhead and rattler ranging northward into Canada.

Contrary to popular belief, rattlesnakes don't have to be coiled to strike, nor do they always buzz a warning of their intentions. Exercise caution when handling a dead one, which can harm even after death, due to nerve reflex action.

The punctures of pit vipers should be sliced open and the poison removed by means of the suction cup contained in snake-bite kits. Lacking one of these, it can be done by mouth, providing it's free of sores or cuts.

A tourniquet should be applied between the wound and the heart. Victims should avoid exertion so the poison doesn't spread due to increased blood circulation. Alcoholic beverages should also be shunned and professional medical attention quickly found.

Scalds and burns should not be regarded lightly. Serious sunburns result from reflection off a lake's surface. Cold water provides relief, but those of a serious nature should be treated by a doctor. Shock is a dangerous side-effect of scalds and second or third-degree burns.

The poisonous oak, ivy and sumac plants are easily identified, and every outdoorsman should learn to recognize them and give a wide berth. Burning them is one of the surest ways to become infected, the smoke being highly toxic. Calamine lotion is a recommended treatment.

Pills rate inclusion in the fisherman's first-aid kit. To be effective, those to counteract motion sickness — in the air or on the sea — should be swallowed in advance of the situation. If any doubts shadow the pure qualities of available drinking water, boil or treat with halazone tablets before drinking. The causes of diarrhea are often water-borne. The other extreme is constipation. Lack of regularity is a common complaint among fishermen on extended outings. It's often due to a break from the normal daily pattern. Changes in time-zones, food and liquid can all be contributing factors. There are many patented products for easing the problem, all to be taken in moderate dosages.

Most headaches while on the waters result from heat and glare. Polaroid sunglasses pay off by helping avert nagging, painful headaches and smarting eyes. By eliminating surface glare, the fisherman can spot underwater snags, boulders, and even fish.

Codeine pills usually cure discomfort of headaches and provide temporary relief from toothaches and other minor pains.

Fishing drownings account for a heavy yearly loss of life, and non-swimmers flirt with death by venturing forth from shore without the protection of a life preserver. Less bulky, and nearly as safe, are those fishing vests and jackets with built-in flotation.

Lightning claims numerous victims annually. Get off the lake during an electrical storm, but don't seek shelter under lone trees in open areas, or the taller ones in a forest. Low, dense foilage offers the safest protection.

Cuts are common in the outdoors, with few severe enough to warrant professional medical attention. Bleeding can usually be arrested by applying firm pressure to the wound. Clean and sterilize the cut before bandaging.

Many a fishing trip has been terminated by a fish hook embedded in the anatomy. Hands, neck and face are obviously the most vulnerable. Hooks can usually be removed with a firm hand plus intestinal fortitude. Push them onwards until the barb projects through the skin. Cut it off, then back the shank out again. Subsequent bleeding usually cleanses the wound, but an anti-tetanus shot is prudent insurance.

In the event of fractures, splint the break firmly and don't move the patient unless necessary. Get him to a hospital as quickly as possible. If isolated from civilization, try to attract assistance with international distress signals.

Most regions are kept under surveillance from fire-towers, and a huge smudge fire — preferably kindled on an island — will likely result in the prompt appearance of a float plane or helicopter. A first-aid kit and a booklet covering temporary treatment for a myriad of maladies and afflictions should reside permanently in tackle box or pack sack.

Always inform companions of your ailments and allergies, especially should certain drugs induce violent and dangerous reactions. In the outdoors, the imagined dangers can be ballooned out of proportion by trepid minds. The real ones are few and far between.

Chapter 17

The Vanishing World

Scientists conducting research into organisms which inhabit the harbor at Toronto, Canada, have warned field workers to get anti-tetanus shots from the nearest hospital should they accidentally cut themselves and use harbor water to wash off the blood.

Water skiing and wading are about to be banned in the Potomac River in the District of Columbia.

Lake Erie is now a sick joke.

Logging operations and water diversion projects in the Pacific northwest are dramatically altering the habits of Pacific salmon.

The Canadian province of Quebec is about to engage in one of the world's largest power projects, diverting many of the rivers which pour into Hudson and James Bays, thereby delivering a death blow to the fragile ecology of that section of the country.

Enough?

Apparently not. Our society continues to plunge headlong on a path of self destruction taking with us the fish and game of the continent. Visiting some of the more remote fishing camps in the U.S. and Canada can be a mind-bending experience, as the angler wades through broken glass, non-deteriorating pop cans, polluting plastics and the other junk that careless, thoughtless anglers and hunters leave behind.

The national surge of interest in conservation in the late Sixties came not a moment too soon, and perhaps several moments too late. Some ecologists say the clock cannot now be turned back; that we have set loose an industrial juggernaut which cannot be stopped, and which will overtake us before remedial measures work.

Mercury and DDT poisoning is now being documented through-out the world. Species of fish and fowl in the far reaches of the

Arctic, presumably out of reach of the industrialized sectors, have shown traces of these pollutants.

Legislators, in the snail-like pace we have come to expect, are finally taking what appears to be vigorous action. Laws with teeth, hopefully not decaying at birth, are being passed from one end of the nation to the other. Whether the cumulative effect will reverse the trend will have to await the next few generations.

But there is a vital role for each and every angler. Here is a brief list: Don't toss trash through ice-fishing holes, or over the stern of your motorboat. Don't throw away "trash fish" at the end of the day. Those "minnows" may carry a disease foreign to the lake, or may include the fry of carp or other undesirable species which could alter and seriously affect the ecology of the region. Remember nature can recover from some blows, but it now takes longer and longer and longer. The point is near when certain lakes and rivers will have no power to regenerate. Scorn companions who leave a campsite filled with debris, leaving it to the "next" man to clean up. The next man may never have the chance to come along.

More and more government agencies are joining the battle to keep the environment clean. Cooperate with them. Use the many receptacles which now dot the nation. Save garbage, even if you have to carry it for miles, for proper disposal. Support the campaigns various states have instituted for boating with electric motors only. Noise pollution is just as formidable as chemical and visual pollution. Insist when you buy outboards, snowmobiles, motorcycles or all-terrain vehicles that they have the maximum muffler capacity, and press for development of engines which operate more efficiently. Leave the blaring transistor radio at home. Fishing is essentially a peaceful pursuit — if you will let it be.

Chapter 18

Appetizing Aftermath

Even if your catch isn't worthy of a snapshot, culinary consolation is an excellent salve.

Fish recipes are myriad, and when complemented by the cook's imagination, each fish-feed can be differently delicious. Add onion, bayleaf, a dash of thyme, oregano or whatever spice is handy. And black olives, mushrooms, or wine will give an ordinary dish the "gourmet touch".

There are numerous cooking methods, usually influenced by size, species, and personal preference. One important factor predominates: do not overcook! This toughens the flesh, and no amount of "dressing up" can disguise dry, leathery texture.

Whole fish and very thick cuts are ideal for baking — "as is" or stuffed. Fatty fish, such as shad, respond deliciously to this method. Bake in a hot oven, a good rule-of-thumb being 10 minutes of cooking time per inch of thickness.

Lean fish and small fillets of fat fish should be braised. This is best done by wrapping the fish in tinfoil with a little stock or court-bouillon and baking in a moderate oven.

Broiling or grilling is fine with certain species. Fish done in this manner may be whole, split or filleted. If the fillets are small, or you suspect the flesh may dry out, baste often with a little butter or oil, adding a squeeze of lemon.

Deep-frying is popular, but first bring the oil or lard to the correct temperature. If the pan is not hot enough, the end result will be a greasy, soggy offering instead of a memorable meal. From 360° to 380° is recommended, and adding a few fish at a time will prevent lowering of temperature. Batter is a favorite, but fish may be rolled in bread or cracker crumbs, and even household flour, having first been dipped in an egg-and-milk mixture.

The panfrying method is not confined to the kitchen, and is a great way to cook your catch in camp. Small, whole fish or fillets are best suited. That fat should be hot, but not smoking, and juicier results are achieved by cooking over medium heat. Dip the fish in seasoned milk, then roll in cornmeal, flour or bread crumbs.

Subtle poaching brings out the delicate flavour of species such as salmon. The golden rule here is to never boil it. To keep it intact, wrap cheesecloth around the fish prior to placing it in the pot. Stocks used in this method run the gamut from milk and water, to fish stock, to vegetable with the addition of a small quantity of wine.

Camping in hot weather can present storage problems for perishables such as butter. And if you've overlooked cooking oil on your check list, don't despair. Fillets are delicious when dusted with pepper and salt and sprinkled liberally with lemon juice. Wrap them tightly in tinfoil and place in the glowing embers of the fire. Leave for about 20 minutes, carefully remove the package and test the flesh with a fork. If it flakes easily, it's ready for eating.

If your catch is too large to consume immediately, or you've hit a piscatorial jackpot, freezing is the answer. This must be done carefully. Otherwise, freezer-burn and/or dryness will spoil your anticipated pleasure. One excellent mode of freezing small whole fish and fillets is in a waxed milk or milk-shake container. Simply fill the carton with water, stick a piece of wire through the tail portion of the fish and suspend it, completely immersed, in the water. The surrounding block of ice precludes any possibility of burning and drying.

Many people refuse to eat fish, rating it a poor second to meat. However, properly cooked and garnished it's far from mundane and can take its rightful place as gourmet fare.

Chapter 19

The Freshwater Fish Of North America

ARCTIC GRAYLING

One of North America's most beautiful and sought-after fish, this distinctive and delicate creature has lured many adventuresome anglers to the icy northern waters. Except for token appearance in U.S. rivers, except Alaska, the grayling is located almost exclusively in the Arctic watershed.

Spawning Habits

The Arctic grayling spawns from March to June in small, swiftly-flowing rivers. The male repels invaders and it is interesting to note that his majestic dorsal fin is held erect during these encounters. After a few weeks the eggs hatch and the fry feed voraciously.

Appearance

It is in this category that the Arctic grayling achieves true distinction. The most notable feature, of course, is its beautiful sail-like dorsal fin, supported by 17 or more rays, colored greyish-black with a red or pink band along the upper edge. This fin also carries large blue spots. The main background color of the fish itself varies enormously from lake to lake and even within a lake or river. The range is from dark blue or purple on the back, to grey, silver or brown. From the gills back half way are dark splotches, sometimes blue, which resemble ditto marks. When the sun is right, the fish appears to have a gold sheen, like some armor-plated knight seeking the Holy Grail. This sheen vanishes after exposure to the air. In the male, the first part of the mighty dorsal is highest with the reverse being true of the female.

Angling Tips

Anglers will find a number of contradictions in material about the Arctic grayling, the most pronounced being about the tenderness of its mouth to the hook. Many anglers have reported apparent tearing of the mouth from a badly fixed hook, but what may be the trouble is that the Arctic grayling has a small mouth and it takes a keen sense of timing to set the hook correctly.

The grayling tends to run in schools, and while oblivious to the angler, will nonetheless think twice about rising to a badly presented fly.

It is capricious and will at different times take the most awkwardly presented fly instantly, or lurk about, testing the angler's patience and his supply of flies.

The best way to approach a school of grayling holding their position on the bottom is to cast downstream so that the fly is the first thing they see. They may ignore many offerings before taking one, and they usually take it behind their holding position.

At certain and unpredictable occasions, the grayling will rise from the bottom and execute a beautiful leap, seeming to sail over and take the fly on the return. While fly-fishing for grayling tests the angler's skill to the utmost, spinning with a variety of lures can bring good results.

Fly fishermen should include in their tackle boxes a selection of Dark Cahill, Black Ant, Grey and Brown Hackles, Ginger Quill, and Stone Fly with No. 10, 12 and 14 hooks.

ARCTIC GRAYLING

State or Province	Frequency	Average Size lbs.-ozs.	Record lbs.-ozs.	Year
Alaska	abundant	—	4 – 0	1967
CANADA				
Alberta	present	1 – 0	2 – 13	1966
British Columbia	present	1 – 0	—	—
Manitoba	present	—	3 – 2	1970
N.W. Territories	abundant	2 – 0	5 – 15	1967
Saskatchewan	abundant	1 – 8	4 – 5	1966
Yukon Territories	abundant	1 – 8	—	—

MUSKELLUNGE

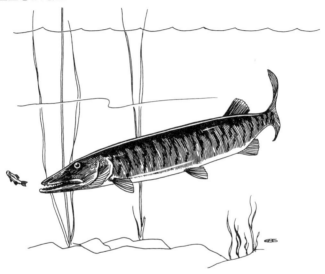

Other names: This North American member of the pike family is also called maskinonge (derived from two Indian words meaning deformed pike), mascalonge, muskallonge, the great pike, tiger musky, the lunge, the Great Lakes maskinonge, and most commonly, the musky.

Controversy still swirls and eddies about this fierce game fish, unique to North America, but despite its critics the musky provides the most exciting and vigorous fresh water sport fishing on the continent.

The controversy surrounding the musky and its relative, the northern pike, grew from the predatory nature of the fish. Apart from devouring at an enormous rate other small fresh water companions including bass, carp, trout, frogs, perch, suckers, shiners, this sullen creature has been found with ducklings, muskrats, mice and even birds in its interior.

Tales have been circulated that the musky attacks humans not unlike the shark, however discount this as idle talk and think of this great fish as an exciting and wary adversary whose only danger lies in the rows of sharp teeth which can slice the angler who fails to dispose of it quickly after boating it.

Spawning Habits

The musky spawns early in the spring at a time dictated by temperature, the most common element of nature controlling this phenomenon. The temperature must reach about 50 degrees before spawning takes place. The musky selects shallow, quiet areas of lakes and rivers. They move in pairs and from time to time turn on their sides to emit milt and eggs simultaneously and randomly. This activity may last from five days to two weeks depending on the temperature.

Appearance

The musky is generally larger and longer than a northern pike and can be distinguished by two essential features, coloring and scaling. In the musky, there are many square or round black spots or stripes along the sides against a sliver-like or grey background, fading to a light belly. In the pike, the background color is dark. The cheeks of the pike are fully scaled, while on the musky, only the top half is scaled.

The musky has a long, lean body with its anal and dorsal fins close to the tail. Its weight averages about 10 pounds but the commercial fishing record is 110 pounds for a giant caught in a Michigan lake back in 1915. It was 7 feet 4 inches long and measured a striking 51 inches around the middle.

Angling Tips

Admiring its size and sporting qualities is one thing, catching it is another. Serious musky fishermen often wait days and weeks to land one. The fish has been described as "tricky" and "sullen" because of the unpredictable nature of its response to a lure. Among the many things affecting its performance on any given day is the availability of other fish in the neighborhood to assuage its voracious appetite.

The best fishing for musky is in the fall, because in July and August it withdraws from its spawning grounds to deeper waters.

When the leaves start to turn in September and October the mysterious musky moves to shallower waters, lying alongside logs, or in lily pads, weed beds, or along the shoreline by submerged rocks.

Pick an overcast day with the surface of the water ruffled by the wind. Make sure your tackle is strong enough, because while you might not care a twit about losing it, losing the fish by being under-equipped is more frustrating.

You can troll, cast or stillfish, and a nylon line testing at least 20 pounds is recommended. If trolling, the angler should use a stout trolling rod 5 to 6 feet in length and mounted with a heavy-duty star-drag reel. For casting or stillfishing, casting rods or two handed surf rods with plenty of backbone are ideal. Always use a wire leader to forestall the musky's sharp teeth severing the line. Large lures and infinite patience are needed to land the musky. Once sure of a hit, strike back quickly to imbed the hook firmly in the creature's hard mouth. If you prefer bait such as suckers or yellow perch, release any pressure on the line after a strike, because the musky will "mouth" the bait, swim away to a secluded corner where it turns the bait around until it is going down head first. This can take up to 20 minutes if the bait is sizeable. But once the bait is swallowed, "sock it to him" to implant the hooks firmly.

Some of the top musky plugs are over a foot in length, are extremely productive and thus popular with anglers. They are usually constructed of plastic or wood.

Aimless trolling may bring sucecss if you have enough patience and persistence, but if you are trying for musky for the first time, see what the local guides say about the best spots.

Once hooked, the musky exhibits all the anger of a wounded tiger, lunging and twisting for freedom. It possesses great endurance. It will leap from the water, thrashing wildly, and it is during this thrilling moment you can see the wide open mouth and the rows of sharp teeth. The musky may then dive to the bottom, cruise slowly, and contemplate its next move, or it may head quickly for line-snaring sunken logs. A taut line is absolutely essential to land this beauty. Finally as you see the white underbelly twisting in its final agonies, reel the musky in. Using a gaff or a net — and with the line always taut — bring the fish into the boat and club it between the eyes, because many a musky has been lost even at this final moment. Experienced musky anglers keep a heavy leather glove handy for the final rituals.

Landing a 30 pound musky is one of fishing's finest moments; plan for it carefully.

MUSKELLUNGE

State or Province	Frequency	Average Size lbs.-ozs.	Record lbs.-ozs.	Year
Arkansas	present	—	—	—
Indiana	present	—	12 – 0	1965
Iowa	present	—	23 – 2	1971
Kentucky	present	10 – 0	39 – 14	1969
Maryland	present	10 – 0	31 – 8¾	1966
Massachusetts	present	—	—	—
Michigan	abundant	10 – 0	62 – 8	1940
Minnesota	present	15 – 0	56 – 8	—
Missouri	present	—	14 – 8	1969
Nebraska	present	—	18 – 4	1969
New Jersey	present	—	19 – 0	1971
New York	present	—	69 – 15	1957
North Carolina	present	—	—	—
North Dakota	present	10 – 0	20 – 0	—
Ohio	present	12 – 0	44 – 0	1971
Oklahoma	present	—	—	—
Pennsylvania	abundant	—	54 – 3	1924
Tennessee	present	10 – 0	33 – 0	1971
Vermont	present	6 – 0	23 – 8	1970
Virginia	present	—	29 – 0	—
West Virginia	present	12 – 0	43 – 0	1955
Wisconsin	abundant	8 – 0	69 – 11	1949
CANADA				
Manitoba	present	—	—	—
Ontario	abundant	8 – 0	61 – 9	—
Quebec	present	10 – 0	50 – 0	1957

NORTHERN PIKE

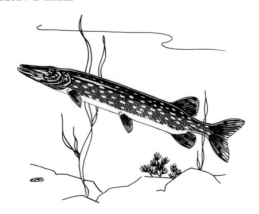

Other names: This cousin to the musky is found around the world in the northern climes and is also known as the grass pike, the Jackpike, the common pike, and in the north, the Jackfish. Living under the same dislikes that afflict the musky, the northern pike is nonetheless an excellent game fish, clean and when taken in colder waters extremely flavorsome.

The distaste for them was harbored by natives of an area who attributed the decline in other fish to the predatory nature of the northern pike. But in the long run, the balance of nature has resulted in other fish co-existing with the northern pike as the East seems to be doing with the West, uneasily but so far successfully.

Spawning Habits

As with the musky, the northern pike spawn in the early spring after the ice breaks. The female will seek out shallow marshy waters, close to shore, or quiet rivers, and broadcast her eggs randomly to be fertilized by the accompanying male or males. Spawning begins in the third or fourth years of life and up to a half a million eggs can be laid by one medium sized pike. The fry — if they miss being devoured or exposed by receding waters — eat anything around, including smaller fry. The average weight of pike taken is about 3 pounds but 20 pounders are not uncommon.

Appearance

The northern pike is long, lean and slender with bulging alligator-like jaws filled with long, sharp teeth. It can be distinguished from its surly relative, the musky, by its generally smaller size, different coloring and scaling. The basic background color is dark and the markings are light. The background color varies from greyish blue to green and the markings are usually white or off-white spots, ovals or oblongs running horizontally. Scales fully cover the cheeks and the top half of the gill covers. Anal and dorsal fins lie close to the tail and are all marked with prominent dark spots.

Angling Tips

As with the musky, the fall is the best time to catch a pike. But either in spring or fall, close to shore during the daytime is the best bet. Whether myth or fact, successful anglers report that cloudy, windy days are the most fruitful. Like the musky, the pike hides and lurks in weed beds, near logs and overhangs, around sunken stumps or lily pads. In lakes, they seek out coves, reefs, the edge of sand bars and inlets and outlets to the lake. When feeding, they are close to the surface but go deeper when resting.

You can easily fool the pike in Northern virgin waters, but in popular areas it takes work to land one. You can choose your method with pike, either spinfishing, casting, stillfishing, trolling or icefishing. But whatever way, make sure you have at least 6 inches of wire leader at the end of your line, for the pike's sharp teeth can sever the toughest nylon. When casting or spinning, use bright spoons, or spinners, surface or underwater plugs. Make sure when casting you get the most from your lure by changing the speed of the retrieve. When trolling, large spinners with feathered hooks are productive.

Be prepared for the strike, because the pike smashes the lure hard and fast. Set the hook well since its jaws are as tough as the musky's. Shifting from lures to bait, you can use frogs, suckers, perch or large minnows. Small pike leap from the water frequently but the larger pike do their fighting under water. They can fool you by coming in to the boat only to lunge when you think you have them, catching you off guard and perhaps snapping the line.

In the case of the northern pike, you don't have to wait until its white underbelly shows as long as it's fully played out. Once boated, club it between the eyes, being careful of the teeth.

NORTHERN PIKE

State or Province	Frequency	Average Size lbs.-ozs.	Record lbs.-ozs.	Year
Alaska	abundant	—	27 – 8	1969
Arizona	present	—	16 – 13	1970
Arkansas	present	3 – 0	8 – 1	1969
Colorado	present	8 – 0	23 – 12	1969
Connecticut	present	4 – 8	16 – 11	1960
Illinois	present	4 – 0	20 – 2	1952
Indiana	present	—	20 – 12	1964
Iowa	abundant	—	23 – 8	1970
Kansas	present	4 – 0	24 – 12	1971
Maryland	present	4 – 0	19 – 4	1970
Massachusetts	present	—	24 – 8	1967
Michigan	abundant	3 – 0	33 – 8	1969
Minnesota	abundant	2 – 8	45 – 2	—
Missouri	present	—	9 – 9	1971
Montana	present	—	—	—
Nebraska	present	—	27 – 8	1962
Nevada	present	5 – 0	10 – 10	1971
New Hampshire	present	5 – 0	16 – 1	1967
New Jersey	present	—	21 – 0	1970

State or Province	Frequency	Average Size lbs.-ozs.	Record lbs.-ozs.	Year
New Mexico	present	3 – 8	30 – 0	1970
New York	abundant	—	46 – 2	1940
North Dakota	abundant	3 – 8	37 – 8	1968
Ohio	present	9 – 0	14 – 6	1961
Oklahoma	present	3 – 0	14 – 10	1969
Pennsylvania	present	—	19 – 0	1970
Rhode Island	present	—	19 – 0	1970
South Dakota	abundant	—	33 – 8	—
Texas	present	4 – 0	—	—
Utah	present	—	—	—
Vermont	present	3 – 0	26 – 0	1970
Virginia	present	—	17 – 0	—
West Virginia	present	4 – 8	8 – 0	1971
Wisconsin	abundant	3 – 0	38 – 0	1952
Wyoming	present	2 – 0	—	—
CANADA				
Alberta	abundant	4 – 0	32 – 0	1948
British Columbia	present	10 – 0	30 – 0	—
Manitoba	abundant	—	41 – 2	1969
Newfoundland	abundant	5 – 0	—	—
N.W. Territories	abundant	5 – 0	41 – 0+	—
Ontario	abundant	4 – 0	42 – 2	—
Quebec	abundant	7 – 0	45 – 15	1964
Saskatchewan	abundant	—	42 – 12	1954
Yukon Territories	abundant	8 – 0	—	—

CHAIN PICKEREL

Other names: There are three general species of pickerel; the chain pickerel, the grass or mud pickerel and the redfin. The chain pickerel is also known as pike, banded pickerel, common pickerel, grass pike, green pike, chain pike, and jack pike.

Despite this unwieldy and confusing collection of names, this smaller member of the pike family does provide entertainment and satisfactory eating.

It is not as attractive to sport fishermen as its two bigger and more vigorous cousins, but it is more of a game fish than say perch. If skinned rather than scaled it can be tasty.

Spawning Habits

A spring spawner like the pike and musky, the pickerel scatters its eggs over shallow areas randomly, preferring weed beds and marshy areas. The fry grow quickly and move from insects to frogs, crayfish and occasionally small birds for sustenance.

Appearance

While there is some confusion between the chain pickerel and the northern pike, the chain pickerel is usually smaller and much less fearsome a fighter. The distinguishing features are a dark green or brownish back, shading to a lighter green on the sides, over which is superimposed a chain-like dark marking giving rise to the name. The bellies are light or white in color. A number of hybrids occur so that any description must contain the words "some of the time." For example, both the gill covers and cheeks are scaled most of the time, but exceptions occur.

The "little pickerels", the grass or redfin pickerels are smaller than the chain pickerel and the redfin occurs primarily in the St. Lawrence River. Both carry dark wavy lines as opposed to the chain-like marking of the chain pickerel.

Angling Tips

Small spoons in any color are practical, or various weighted spinners. Fly fishermen can use popping bugs. Natural bait such as frogs, shiners or chubs can be used with success.

This fish lends itself to ice-fishing, but the best times during the rest of the year are April to June and September and October. The chain pickerel averages about two pounds. The most popular gear are the fly or spinning rods.

Remember that as with the larger and more exciting members of this family, let the pickerel have a chance to mouth the bait. It may take it and swim for several yards before swallowing it and that's time to set the hook.

Try all the shallow spots first, near dead trees, logs, and muddy or sandy stretches, and in lily pads or near rocks. During the summer heat, try trolling in deeper water with a spoon or spinner.

Pickerel meat is bony and sweet and responds best to pan frying.

CHAIN PICKEREL

State or Province	Frequency	Average Size lbs.-ozs.	Record lbs.-ozs.	Year
Alabama	abundant	0 – 8	5 – 8	1971
Arkansas	abundant	1 – 0	5 – 0	1971
Connecticut	abundant	2 – 8	7 – 14	1969
Delaware	present	—	—	—
Florida	present	—	—	—
Georgia	abundant	2 – 0	9 – 6	1961
Louisiana	abundant	—	—	—
Maine	abundant	3 – 0	6 – 8	1969
Maryland	abundant	1 – 0	7 – 9	1970
Massachusetts	abundant	—	9 – 5	1954
Michigan	present	—	—	—
Mississippi	present	1 – 8	4 – 4	—
Missouri	present	—	—	—
Nebraska	present	—	—	—
New Hampshire	abundant	1 – 8	8 – 0	1966
New Jersey	abundant	—	9 – 3	1957
New York	abundant	—	—	—
North Carolina	abundant	1 – 0	8 – 0	1968
Ohio	present	3 – 0	6 – 4	1961
Oklahoma	present	0 – 8	—	—
Pennsylvania	abundant	—	8 – 0	1937
Rhode Island	abundant	1 – 8	6 – 8	1969
South Carolina	abundant	1 – 8	6 – 0	1962
Tennessee	present	0 – 8	5 – 12	1951
Texas	present	1 – 0	—	—
Vermont	present	1 – 8	3 – 11	1969
Virginia	abundant	—	7 – 11	—
West Virginia	present	0 – 8	4 – 1	1970

CANADA

New Brunswick	abundant	2 – 0	—	—
Nova Scotia	present	0 – 8	—	—
Quebec	present	2 – 8	8 – 0	1960
Saskatchewan	present	—	—	—

THE SALMON AND TROUT FAMILIES

If the streams, lakes, rivers and oceans of North America have any distinction it is for the various elegant members of the trout and salmon families; from the Atlantic to the Pacific salmon, from the rainbow to the brook trout, this family of fish provides a rare combination of skill and taste for every kind of fisherman.

There are three main sub-groups in the Salmonidae family, which will be dealt with in order.

1. Salmo, which includes Atlantic salmon, rainbow trout, Kamloops trout, mountain Kamloops and mountain cut-throat trout, brown trout, coastal cut-throat and steelhead trout.

2. Salvelinus, which includes brook, wendigo, and lake trout and the famed Dolly Varden and Arctic char.

3. Oncorhynchus, which includes pink salmon, sockeye salmon, kokanee salmon, chum, chinook and coho salmon.

Group One
ATLANTIC SALMON

The world's most exciting, most revered fresh water fish is the famed Atlantic salmon. Apart from its stirring qualities as a fighter, it is also a culinary delight, and has lured tens of thousands of sportsmen to the east coast to angle for this prize.

Travelling to the east coast was not always necessary for this great fish. Many citizens once fished for this salmon inland. But industrialization, the onslaught of chemical pollutants and early fish mismanagement killed off the Atlantic salmon, and by the turn of the century conservation attempts had failed.

But there are still more than 300 rivers in Maine, Connecticut, Massachusetts, New York, New Brunswick, Nova Scotia, Quebec, Newfoundland and Labrador where this beauty can be caught.

Spawning Habits

Salmon spend most of their time at sea but travel up freshwater streams and rivers to spawn. The Atlantic salmon leaves the sea and enters the river from the early spring to the late fall, guided only by temperature and flow of the stream. The temperature and flow are usually better in the spring and fall, concentrating the runs during these periods. The Atlantic salmon will try to find its way back to its original place of birth but adverse conditions can direct it elsewhere.

The female salmon creates a nest by digging with her tail in the gravel or small stones of a river. After eggs and sperm are dropped the female covers the nest. This act may be repeated up to eight times, each time moving upstream. After a long incubation period, 100 to 200 days depending on temperature, the alevin as they are called, appear. After the alevin consumes its yolk sac it is called a parr until it returns to the sea which may be from one to three years. At this point they are called smolts and are about six inches long. After one year at sea they are called grilse and weigh now from three to five pounds. Some grilse return to spawn immediately but they usually stay one to two more years in salt water before returning. An Atlantic salmon may spawn as many as three times.

Appearance

Returning from the sea, the Atlantic salmon has a bright steely-blue back, silvery sides and a light belly. Spots and little X-marks are found on the top and sides. The flesh is pink. After a short while in fresh water, the steel-blue color gives way to a reddish grey. The tail is deeply forked. The parr are distinguished by large, rectangular dark marks, 10 or 11 of them, which run vertically along the sides from gills to tail. The average weight on returning from the sea is 12 to 15 pounds, but catches of 20 to 30 pounds are not uncommon.

Angling Tips

The best fishing occurs during May and June when the spring run is on, although in the fall the water boils with action at river mouths as the anxious salmon start the trek inland. It is at these times you can see the graceful and spectacular leaps by these active creatures as they head ever farther up river. Regulations are usually rigid and catching the Atlantic salmon is permitted in certain seasons and with fly only. To your single-action reel should be attached 150 to 200 yards of backing, testing at between 15 to 20 pounds. Experts will wrangle for hours about the best flies to catch salmon with, but a good selection of wets would include Black Rose, and Jock Scott. Dry flies to be carried include Pink Lady and the various spiders. Hooks generally should range from No. 8 to No. 6/0. Leaping salmon are not as likely to take the fly as salmon resting behind or beside rocks in the swift current. They also lurk around gravel bars or tails of pools, along banks or ledges. Cast across or downstream, letting the fly drift as normally as possible. It should be presented broadside to the fish if at all feasible.

Because of the enormous variation in runs in different rivers, it is wise to consult a guide. In some places, when fly fishing from a boat for Atlantic salmon, a guide is mandatory. It will save many hours of fruitless casting by getting the right help at the right time.

The salmon takes the fly in a deliberate manner, so wait a moment before setting the hook. Once hooked, the salmon will give you a fight of your life; it will leap clear of the water, twisting and turning, then make a long run, usually downstream. Keep a light drag on the reel and try to keep even with the fish as it makes its moves. Let it take the line freely, always watching for an attempt to escape over a difficult series of rapids.

Fly rods from 7½ to 9½ feet are most common now, although longer and heavier two-handed rods are still used. The smaller the river, the lighter should be the rod. And the lower and clearer the river, the smaller the fly should be.

ATLANTIC SALMON

State or Province	Frequency	Average Size lbs.-ozs.	Record lbs.-ozs.	Year
Connecticut	present	—	—	—
Maine	present	12 – 0	26 – 2	1959
Massachusetts	present	—	8 – 1	1971
New Hampshire	present	—	—	—
New York	present	—	—	—
Vermont	present	—	—	—
CANADA				
New Brunswick	abundant	5 – 0	—	—
Newfoundland	abundant	—	—	—
Nova Scotia	present	—	52 – 8	1927
Prince Edward Is.	present	—	23 – 14	1970
Quebec	present	10 – 0	42 – 0	1960

LANDLOCKED SALMON

Other names: ouananiche, lake salmon, sebago salmon.

This relative of the Atlantic salmon duplicates the appeal of its cousin and lacks only its sea-going traits, hence the appropriate name.

Spawning Habits

Similar to the Atlantic salmon, without the sea-going activity.

Appearance

The major difference apart from size (the ouananiche is generally smaller than the Atlantic salmon), is the double-X marks on the back and sides and the slightly darker background color. The blue-green tapers off to a silvery color tinged with red.

Angling Tips

Following spring break-up is the peak time to seek out this vigorous and spectacular game fish. In spring, when the lake runs cold, is the time to cast for them, although one can troll effectively as well. Pick a medium to heavy fly rod and match it with your favorite wet or streamer fly. If trolling, use streamers such as the Black or Grey Ghost. Spoons and spinners are also effective. For anglers trying natural bait, drift-fish with minnows or dead smelt. When the ice breaks, the ouananiche moves to the inlets and the shore line to feed on bait fish moving upstream to spawn. When warmer weather comes in July and August, they retreat further underwater and are only reachable by deep trolling with a metal line. Only in the fall do they return to the shores and inlets.

At the peak spring season, a raw day when the water is choppy will bring the ouananiche right to the surface throughout the day. In calmer weather, early or late fishing will likely bring better results.

Some expert anglers prefer casting to trolling but the work is more difficult. When hooked near the surface, the ouananiche strikes hard and fights harder. Better play it until it turns on its side before attempting to boat it, or face the prospect of losing it prematurely. Ouananiche fishing is just about the slowest, least productive angling on the continent, and even dyed-in-the-wool fishers who work at it for countless hours in a season will catch no more than a handful. For them, it's worth it.

LANDLOCKED SALMON

State or Province	Frequency	Average Size lbs.-ozs.	Record lbs.-ozs.	Year
Maine	abundant	2 – 8	22 – 8	1907
New Hampshire	abundant	3 – 0	18 – 8	1942
New York	present	—	16 – 14	1958
Oregon	present	4 – 0	8 – 0	—
Vermont	present	2 – 8	5 – 8	1969
CANADA				
New Brunswick	present	2 – 0	—	—
Newfoundland	abundant	3 – 0	—	—
Nova Scotia	present	—	—	—
Quebec	present	2 – 0	16 – 8	1968
Ontario	present	3 – 0	—	—

RAINBOW TROUT

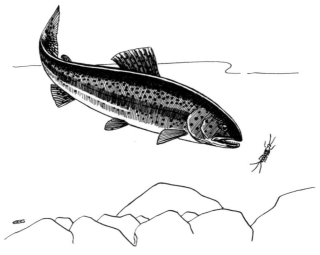

Other names: In a welter of scientific confusion, several facts emerge: There are a lot of rainbows masquerading under other names. Some versions deserve their own chapter, and the most common are discussed here. The species include, steelhead, Kamloops, mountain Kamloops, western rainbow, California trout and Pacific trout.

One expert notes, "The whole group of races comprising the rainbow or steelhead series, with the probable exception of the golden trout, are too alike and too overlapping in their characters to admit the view that any one is completely differentiated from the others."

Whatever the scientific problems in isolating the varieties, the angler has no problem identifying a game fish with outstanding qualities, whether he fishes in the east, the mid-west or Pacific coast regions of the continent.

(In fact the rainbow in its many versions exists around the world from the Andes in South America, to New Zealand, Asia and Africa).

The rainbow is a migratory fish and while the non-sea-going varieties have less ground to retreat to, they nonetheless move swiftly and frequently in the giant rivers and lakes of North America.

STEELHEAD

The steelhead has its origin on the west coast but has been successfully transplanted in many places across the U.S. and Canada. Its fighting qualities have compelled anglers to equate it with the Atlantic salmon.

Spawning Habits

Steelhead usually spawn from February to June in large and small streams. They may enter these rivers well before spawning and experts have identified spring, summer and winter runs.

On a sandy bottom the female digs a redd which can be four or five inches deep and up to two feet long. One or more males pair off with the female who deposits her eggs, then fills in the bed after fertilization. She sometimes moves upstream to make another redd. The eggs incubate in from 3 to 7 months, depending on temperature.

Appearance

The steelhead, like all rainbows, carries black spots, the number and size of which vary from fish to fish. It appears that in many cases the nearness to the surface determines the extent of spotting and the size, the skin of the fish reacting somewhat to sunshine as the vacationing secretary: The more the skin is exposed the darker it gets.

Its general color in the sea is silvery, its caudal fin square and spotted, and its short anal fin distinguishes it from Pacific salmon. When the fish moves into fresh water, the blue cast of the back and upper sides changes to green and a pinkish tinge emerges from the sides around the lateral line. The spots become darker and more noticeable. At spawning time the pink tinge changes to a deep red or purple, and thereby leading to the rainbow appellation.

Angling Tips

Many expert anglers describe the steelhead as the gamest of all freshwater fishes. They rise to the fly in fresh and salt water and when hooked, engage in a spectacular fight, leaping from the water and then taking off in long runs.

Spinning is becoming the most popular way to land the steelhead although stillfishing, fly-fishing and trolling can be effective. Many anglers choose to use waders and fish in or from the banks of swiftly-moving rivers. Bright spoons and spinners are productive and the top bait is salmon or steelhead eggs. The latter are tied in tiny clusters in a fine netting (such as nylon stocking), and attached to the hook. There is a great diversity of runs for this creature and the best way to be assured of a good catch is to consult with local residents and guides about particular rivers.

In some places, there appears to be a continuous run while in others, the run occurs during specific periods. When the water gets too cold, the steelhead tends to be quiet, lying close to the bottom and refusing to respond to the most sophisticated approaches. Also after heavy rains the muddy, swollen waters tend to ruin the fishing. In swiftly running rivers, look for your quarry beside, behind, or just ahead of obstructions, as they take advantage of every submerged water-diverter to stop and rest. If you study the river during low water you'll be armed with know-how for the high water good fishing periods.

KAMLOOPS TROUT

Another version of the rainbow is the mighty Kamloops trout, which has been transplanted successfully in many states.

Spawning Habits

Kamloops spawn in May and June and being essentially inland fish they seek out gravelly beds in the rivers and lakes. It takes almost two months for the eggs to hatch and after that, growth depends on the amount of food available nearby.

Appearance

It closely resembles the steelhead, and, the difference in coloration can confuse even the most dedicated scientist. For the angler, it just becomes a maze. In the larger lakes, they tend to be less heavily spotted than in the rivers. The crimson or reddish band that distinguishes this breed is heightened at the spawning season while the silvery color is predominant at other times. Presumably the shallower the water, the darker become the spots. On the lake variety of Kamloops, the spots are comparatively small and sit above the lateral line. The head, dorsal and caudal fins are spotted while the chin and underjaw are blackish. When the fish approaches spawning time, the lateral band becomes crimson.

Angling Tips

The largest number of Kamloops are taken by trolling, but spinning is moving ahead in popularity. The average catch weighs between 7 and 11 pounds. The Kamloops has been described as a demon when hooked. The fish makes long runs, then will leap from the water, thrashing. And it will keep a reserve of strength for one last fling just when you think it's properly played out and ready to be netted.

The warmer the climate, the better is the fishing at dawn or dusk. When the temperature goes down, middle-of-the-day fishing can bring good results. The Kamloops likes swift rivers, and you can count on better fortune looking near rapids, waterfalls, or white water at the heads and tails of pools.

In the evening when the insects play across the face of the water, a dry fly can frequently bring a Kamloops to the top. Let the fly drift along the surface until a strike, then set the hook quickly and keep the line taut. In the heat of summer, in deep waters, troll with lots of line out making the occasional fast retrieve. Salmon eggs for bait, or small spoons and worms can be effective.

RAINBOW, STEELHEAD, KAMLOOPS TROUT*

State or Province	Frequency	Average Size lbs.-ozs.	Record lbs.-ozs.	Year
Alabama	present	1 – 0	3 – 1	1971
Alaska	abundant	—	42 – 2	1970
Arizona	abundant	—	21 – 5½	1966
Arkansas	abundant	0 – 12	16 – 2	1970
California	abundant	5 – 0	21 – 6	1948
Colorado	abundant	0 – 8	18 – 0	1940
Connecticut	abundant	0 – 10	9 – 7	1962
Georgia	abundant	0 – 10	12 – 14	1966
Idaho	present	—	37 – 0	1947
Illinois	present	0 – 8	16 – 7	1971
Indiana	present	—	14 – 10	1968
Iowa	abundant	—	13 – 8	1968

RAINBOW, STEELHEAD, KAMLOOPS TROUT* (Continued)

State or Province	Frequency	Average Size lbs.-ozs.	Record lbs.-ozs.	Year
Kansas	present	0 – 8	—	—
Kentucky	abundant	0 – 8	13 – 12	1971
Maine	present	—	—	—
Maryland	present	0 – 6	27¼"	1959
Massachusetts	present	—	8 – 4	1966
Michigan	abundant	3 – 8	22 – 3	—
Minnesota	abundant	0 – 4	15 – 7	—
Missouri	present	1 – 0	13 – 15	1970
Montana	abundant	—	—	—
Nebraska	present	—	12 – 8	1968
Nevada	present	0 – 8	13 – 4	1968
New Hampshire	abundant	0 – 8	13 – 0	1953
New Jersey	present	—	8 – 5½	1970
New Mexico	abundant	0 – 8	10 – 0	1945
New York	abundant	—	21 – 0	1946
North Carolina	abundant	0 – 8	14 – 1	1949
North Dakota	abundant	1 – 8	9 – 11	1960
Ohio	present	1 – 0	10 – 8	1951
Oklahoma	abundant	0 – 8	10 – 4	1966
Oregon	abundant	8 – 0	35 – 8	—
Pennsylvania	abundant	—	9 – 8	1961
Rhode Island	present	0 – 8	—	—
South Carolina	abundant	—	—	—
South Dakota	abundant	—	11 – 8	—
Tennessee	abundant	0 – 12	12 – 10	1958
Texas	present	0 – 8	4 – 12	1968
Utah	abundant	0 – 12	—	—
Vermont	abundant	2 – 0	10 – 1	1969
Virginia	abundant	—	9 – 14	—
Washington	abundant	—	33 – 0	1962
West Virginia	abundant	0 – 12	10 – 0	1956
Wisconsin	abundant	1 – 0	18 – 15	1970
Wyoming	abundant	0 – 8	22 – 8	1921

CANADA

State or Province	Frequency	Average Size lbs.-ozs.	Record lbs.-ozs.	Year
Alberta	abundant	1 – 0	15 – 0	1967
British Columbia	abundant	2 – 0	36 – 0	1954
Manitoba	present	—	10 – 6	1963
Newfoundland	present	—	—	—
Nova Scotia	present	—	—	—
Ontario	abundant	3 – 0	18 – 2	1966
Prince Edward Is.	present	—	8 – 2	1965
Quebec	present	1 – 8	13 – 0	1966
Saskatchewan	present	3 – 0	18 – 0	1967
Yukon Territories	present	—	19 – 2	—

*In areas where separate records are kept for the steelhead and Kamloops versions of the rainbow trout, we have selected the largest for the purpose of this chart.

CUTTHROAT TROUT

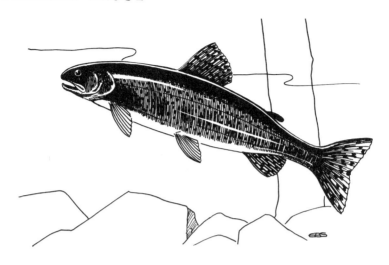

Other names: There are three subspecies to this branch of the family, coastal cutthroat, mountain cutthroat, and Yellowstone cutthroat. Variations in names include Cranbrook trout, lake trout, Snake River cutthroat, and black spotted trout.

There are two essential characteristics that distinguish this breed, a red slash coming from the lower jaw back and upward, and a small patch of teeth on the back of the tongue. Unfortunately for instant recognition, the red slash is not always present and therefore the various subspecies, particularly the coastal cutthroat, are mistaken for steelheads.

Spawning Habits

The coastal cutthroat usually spawns in its fourth year from February to early May. After a couple of years in the stream, the creature will descend to the mouth of the river and stay close by until its spawning time occurs.

Appearance

The sea-going version looks much like the steelhead with its blue-black shiny back and silvery belly. It — and all the other cutthroats — are heavily spotted from gill covers to dorsal and caudal fins. The fresh-water variety has a much wider color pattern and may range from yellowish green to a light orange, to olive-green to dark green. In the fresh water version, the spots on the back and sides may seem to be small crosses or stars.

Angling Tips

The coastal cutthroat is not as game as the rainbow, but it does fight for its freedom and if it loses, is tasty when properly prepared. And while the battle may not be unusual, it may last over a long period. Spin casting with wet or dry flies, or the usual spinners and spoons will bring this fish to the table. While the fighting may not be as thrilling, the beauty of the fish gives added enticement to the angler.

CUTTHROAT TROUT

State or Province	Frequency	Average Size lbs.-ozs.	Record lbs.-ozs.	Year
Alaska	abundant	—	6 – 2	1969
Arizona	present	—	6 – 9	1943
California	present	6 – 0	31 – 8	1911
Colorado	abundant	0 – 12	16 – 0	1964
Idaho	present	—	18 – 6	1957
Montana	present	—	—	—
Nevada	present	3 – 0	41 – 0	1925
New Mexico	abundant	0 – 8	2 – 8	1971
North Dakota	present	1 – 0	—	—
Oregon	abundant	0 – 8	4 – 0	—
Utah	abundant	0 – 12	—	—
Washington	present	—	12 – 0	1961
Wyoming	abundant	1 – 8	15 – 0	1959
CANADA				
Alberta	present	2 – 0	9 – 8	1966
British Columbia	abundant	1 – 0	—	—
Yukon Territories	present	—	—	—

YELLOWSTONE AND MOUNTAIN CUTTHROAT

Of these two, the Yellowstone is by far the more attractive fish to the angler. The Yellowstone, while resembling the Kamloops trout, is also its victim. In water inhabited by both, the Yellowstone usually gives way to the Kamloops. But where it does exist plentifully, it is a livelier fish than its coastal cousin. The Yellowstone will respond to a variety of lures and a catch of 1 to 2 pounds is considered satisfactory.

The Mountain cutthroat, restricted to the headwaters of British Columbia rivers, is no less a fighter than the Yellowstone but certainly less well-known.

BROWN TROUT

Other names, von Behr trout, Loch Leven trout, German brown trout, English brown trout, or simply, brownie.

This canny foreigner was imported to this continent first from Germany (hence von Behr) then from Scotland (Loch Leven) and finally from England.

It was first introduced to Northern American waters in 1891 when eggs were planted at Lac Brulé, Quebec.

Of all the varieties of salmon and trout, this one is probably the most difficult to catch, for it learns quickly and bites infrequently. Therefore it is understandable that novices just don't want to spend the time that an expert is prepared to take to land one.

There is quite a body of myth building up around the brownie, and a number of experts are attempting to establish the point that the more intelligent survive longer and hence propagate a superior breed. Whatever the truth to this theory, the brown trout is demonstrably hard to catch.

Spawning Habits

Brownies start migrating to cooler streams and rivers in late October and November. The female digs a pit or series of pits with her tail in the loose, gravelly, bottom. Eggs and milt are released simultaneously, and after each "planting" the female covers up the bed. During the spawning act, males vigorously defend their turf against rivals and enemies. About a month after fertilization the fry emerge and begin eating insects.

Appearance

Generally, the body of the fish is a golden brown with rusty red or orange spots on the sides and black spots along the back, dorsal adipose and tail fins. Colors in the spawning male are most brilliant. The color can vary considerably, with the main background color going from dirty yellow to greenish brown.

Strong teeth can be found on the jaws, roof of the mouth, and tongue. The older the fish, the darker it becomes, and in the male an extended, hooked lower jaw develops. Those taken from the sea have a more silvery coloration. After spending two or three years in streams, the brownie sometimes moves out into the lakes or to the sea.

Angling Tips

Brownies are found in the larger lakes and rivers and while they can and have adjusted to swift waters, look for them in pools where they have chased other fish away, under rocks, logs, overhangs, bridges, etc. In faster moving water they lurk behind current-splitting rocks. They are essentially night feeders and while they can be caught during the day, the evening gives more promise. The season ranges from April to September but the farther north one goes the better the catch during warmer months.

This is a fish that must be approached with caution. With the Atlantic salmon, one can stand overhead without scaring one away; with the brown trout, avoid even disturbing placid waters or casting a shadow. For wet or dry fly fishing, extreme accuracy is necessary. After the cast, make the dry fly skitter across the surface. Try to hit just beyond the brownie and let the fly pass overhead. Many brownies are missed due to slow reflexes. It takes a fisherman's sense to set the hook swiftly after the strike.

Spinners and spoons are used with some success in larger rivers and lakes. In these waters an expertly fished streamer will also yield results. Bait fishers take their share of brownies with skillful presentation of worms and minnows, generally after dark.

They are tenacious battlers and can do a fair amount of surface scrapping although not in the highflying form of steelheads. They are a worthy opponent on the end of a line. And if you land a good five pound brownie mount it; it may be a long time before the next one.

BROWN TROUT

State or Province	Frequency	Average Size lbs.-ozs.	Record lbs.-ozs.	Year
Arizona	present	—	17 – 0	1971
Arkansas	present	6 – 0	28 – 3	1970
California	present	—	25 – 11	1971
Colorado	abundant	0 – 8	23 – 0	1961
Connecticut	abundant	0 – 12	16 – 4	1968
Georgia	abundant	0 – 12	18 – 3	1967
Idaho	present	—	25 – 12	1969
Illinois	present	0 – 8	13 – 5	1971
Indiana	present	—	11 – 0	1970
Iowa	present	—	12 – 14½	1966
Maine	abundant	3 – 0	19 – 7	1958
Maryland	present	0 – 6	13 – 8	1968
Massachusetts	present	—	19 – 10	1966
Michigan	abundant	1 – 0	21 – 8	1969
Minnesota	present	0 – 8	16 – 8	—
Missouri	present	1 – 8	14 – 1	1970
Montana	abundant	—	—	—
Nebraska	present	—	11 – 4	1950
Nevada	present	1 – 0	12 – 0	1968
New Hampshire	abundant	—	—	—
New Jersey	present	—	16 – 11	1964
New Mexico	abundant	0 – 12	18 – 7	1964
New York	abundant	—	21 – 5	1954
North Carolina	abundant	0 – 8	12 – 0	—
North Dakota	present	1 – 8	5 – 15½	1969
Ohio	present	2 – 0	13 – 8	1942
Oregon	present	0 – 12	25 – 0	—
Pennsylvania	abundant	—	24 – 0	1967
Rhode Island	present	0 – 8	—	—
South Carolina	abundant	0 – 12	13 – 4	1961
South Dakota	abundant	—	18 – 3	—
Tennessee	present	0 – 8	26 – 2	1958
Utah	present	—	—	—
Vermont	abundant	2 – 0	10 – 0	1969
Virginia	present	—	11 – 4	—
Washington	present	—	22 – 0	1965
West Virginia	present	0 – 12	16 – 0	—
Wisconsin	abundant	2 – 0	29 – 9	1971
Wyoming	abundant	—	17 – 8	1945
CANADA				
Alberta	present	2 – 0	12 – 5	1939
British Columbia	present	1 – 0	—	—
Manitoba	present	—	7 – 7	1961
New Brunswick	present	—	—	—
Newfoundland	abundant	4 – 0	27 – 10	—
Nova Scotia	abundant	1 – 0	—	—
Ontario	present	2 – 0	14 – 12	1947
Quebec	present	3 – 8	16 – 9	1959
Saskatchewan	present	1 – 8	15 – 8	1951

93

GOLDEN TROUT

Appearance

This is the most spectacular of the salmon-trout families and one of the most beautiful fish anywhere. It is restricted essentially to the higher altitudes of the western coastal range but turns up in unexpected places such as West Virginia. It has a brilliant deep orange lateral stripe superimposed over some 10 or 11 oblong patches. It shades off into yellow on the belly, where there is a bright streak. Above the lateral line there are more, smaller dark spots on a coppery background. The dorsal and caudal fins are spotted while the anal fin is reddish tipped with white and black. It is not difficult to identify.

Angling Tips

While spoons, streamers, and spinners can land this beauty, expert anglers use flies to hook the golden trout. Recommended are small sizes No. 12 to 22 with tiny midge flies. Small dry flies work when the fish is close to the surface while caddis nymph are the favorite underwater. If you land this magnificent fish, cook it right away; it doesn't keep well, and few anglers who travel long distances to get it carry the correct preserving equipment.

GOLDEN TROUT

State or Province	Frequency	Average Size lbs.-ozs.	Record lbs.-ozs.	Year
California	present	0 – 8	9 – 8	1952
Colorado	present	0 – 8	—	—
Idaho	present	—	5 – 2	1958
Montana	present	—	—	—
New Mexico	present	0 – 8	—	—
Oregon	present	0 – 5	1 – 0	—
Utah	present	0 – 8	—	—
Washington	present	—	—	—
West Virginia	present	0 – 12	2 – 2	1968
Wyoming	present	0 – 8	11 – 4	1948
CANADA				
Alberta	present	1 – 0	4 – 7	1965

Group Two

BROOK TROUT

Other names, Eastern brook trout, speckled trout, native trout, mountain trout, square-tail, mud trout, speckled char, red trout and brookies.

A beautiful, sensitive fish, losing way to civilization but none-theless an attractive creature revered by many anglers for its exquisite coloration.

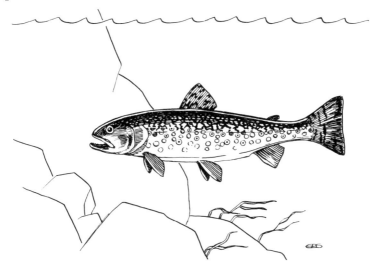

While saddled with the name trout, it is really of the char species and was here even before the Indian claimed the land as his. It offers indomitable fighting spirit, while not being difficult to hook.

Spawning Habits

During October, November and even December, the female brook trout builds her nest in the bottom of streams or shores of shallow lakes, in fairly swift currents. While the female digs out the nest, the male fights off intruders until both are ready; then they swim side by side emitting eggs and milt. The female then covers the nest and moves on to the next nest and repeats this process until exhausted. Incubation varies according to temperature from one month to five months.

Appearance

The brookie usually has a long, slender body, a large mouth and head, teeth on the jaws, tongue and vomer, or bony structure, on the roof of the mouth. Its color varies enormously depending on the location and environment, the color range extending from blue-green to grey-green to olive-green and almost black in salt water. There are wavy, worn-like markings, usually light, on the sides, and below the lateral line many red dots trimmed with blue. The fins, especially the tail fin, are dark and occasionally edged with white.

Angling Tips

In the spring the brook trout becomes ravenous and will hit a wide variety of lures ranging from worms to spinners. It seeks out deep holes, shady spots, it goes underneath waterfalls, hides beside logs, tree roots, log jams and behind rocks and ledges.

A popular way to fish them is with dry or wet flies and, since the fish is essentially an underwater feeder, the wet fly will probably bring you most success, although during insect hatches, dry flies are dynamite.

Don't be surprised if sea-run brookies have a lighter color; they adapt to the environment.

If you're angling with the common garden variety of worm, let it drift along under an overhang, or along the edge of some fast water. Give the fish a moment after the bait is taken before setting the hook, and then be prepared for an excellent fight. The brookie will not leap from the water like its other cousins, but will take short, sharp runs and attempt to foul the line on underwater obstructions. The flesh is usually pink in color and the flavor is excellent.

BROOK TROUT

State or Province	Frequency	Average Size lbs.-ozs.	Record lbs.-ozs.	Year
Alaska	abundant	—	—	—
Arizona	present	—	8 – 3	1943
California	present	0 – 8	9 – 12	1932
Colorado	abundant	0 – 8	7 – 10	1940
Connecticut	abundant	0 – 10	4 – 6	1950
Georgia	present	0 – 4	3 – 12	1969
Idaho	present	—	6 – 10	1958
Illinois	present	0 – 4	4 – 1	1970
Indiana	present	—	1 – 13	1966
Maine	abundant	1 – 0	8 – 5	1958
Maryland	present	0 – 6	23¼″	1967
Massachusetts	abundant	—	—	—
Michigan	abundant	0 – 8	6 – 1	1934
Minnesota	present	0 – 2	9 – 7	—
Montana	abundant	—	—	—
Nebraska	present	—	5 – 1	1965
Nevada	present	0 – 8	5 – 0	1969
New Hampshire	abundant	0 – 8	9 – 0	1911
New Jersey	present	—	6 – 8	1956
New Mexico	abundant	0 – 4	2 – 8	1971
New York	abundant	—	8 – 8	1908
North Carolina	abundant	0 – 4	2 – 8	1966
North Dakota	present	1 – 0	—	—
Ohio	present	1 – 0	2 – 11	1955

State or Province	Frequency	Average Size lbs.-ozs.	Record lbs.-ozs.	Year
Oregon	present	0 – 8	6 – 0	—
Pennsylvania	abundant	—	4 – 4	1966
Rhode Island	present	0 – 8	—	—
South Carolina	present	—	—	—
South Dakota	present	—	5 – 6	—
Tennessee	present	0 – 3	0 – 11	1971
Utah	abundant	0 – 8	—	—
Vermont	abundant	0 – 8	4 – 0	1971
Virginia	abundant	—	3 – 2	1964
Washington	present	—	6 – 3	1970
West Virginia	abundant	0 – 4	3 – 12	1969
Wisconsin	abundant	—	9 – 15	1944
Wyoming	abundant	0 – 2	10 – 0	1933
CANADA				
Alberta	present	1 – 0	12 – 14	1967
British Columbia	present	1 – 0	—	—
Manitoba	present	—	8 – 7	1959
New Brunswick	abundant	2 – 0	—	—
Newfoundland	abundant	2 – 8	—	—
Nova Scotia	abundant	0 – 8	—	—
Ontario	abundant	1 – 8	14 – 8	1915
Prince Edward Is.	abundant	—	8 – 0+	—
Quebec	abundant	0 – 8	11 – 12	1962
Saskatchewan	present	1 – 0	5 – 12	1968

LAKE TROUT

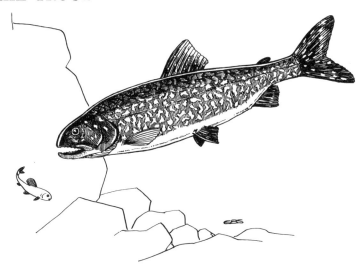

Other names, Great Lakes trout, Great Lakes char, grey trout, Mackinaw, togue, namaycush, salmon trout, landlocked trout, laker and forktail.

97

The lake trout is the largest of the trout family, or more properly the char division of the salmon/trout family. It is a splendid game fish whose essential characteristic is that it prefers the deep, deep lake waters and is usually caught by trolling in the summer months.

Spawning Habits

The spawning period, depending on temperature, extends from mid-September to as late as the end of November. The laker will seek out rocky outcroppings or shoals for spawning and lays its large eggs anywhere from 4 to 6 feet deep. It normally chooses such locations in lakes but may also move up deep rivers. After spawning, lakers abandon the eggs, which take from 4 to 6 months to hatch.

Appearance

There is no mistaking a lake trout. It has a deeply forked tail fin and a large jaw, eyes and mouth. Like many other chars, it has teeth on the jaws, tongue, roof of the mouth, and the middle of the palate has a row of teeth leading back.

The background color is dark ranging from near black through brown to deep green, with grey or white spots lacing the entire superstructure. The belly lightens considerably. Very few lakers have the reddish spots above or below the lateral line, a distinguishing feature of other chars. The color varies from lake to lake.

Angling Tips

In summer, the lake trout is a deepwater fish, seeking out cool and well-oxygenated waters, where herring and whitefish are found. In the smaller lakes, the average catch is between 3 to 5 pounds while in larger lakes the weight goes up to between 10 and 15 pounds.

In the summer, use a metal line for trolling, fishing from 50 feet down. The line should test between 15 and 25 pounds. If you want to be really scientific use a thermometer and troll where the temperature is between 40 to 45 degrees.

It is one of the few trout which are widely fished through the ice during the winter. When spring breakup comes, you may well find the lakers near the surface and then your casting talents can be put into effect. Also in the fall, just before freeze-up they occur in more abundance near the shores and in shallow pools. When hooked near the surface, they put up a good fight, but when one strikes at extreme depths, it is frequently played out even before you bring it to the top.

For ice fishermen, the lake trout is an easy and handy catch, since it frequents all levels looking for food. Its prime source of nourishment includes whitefish, alewives, yellow perch, smelt, and ciscoes.

The lake trout have been the victim of the sea lamprey which until recently was an enormous threat in the Great Lakes (and which led to the creation of the hybrid called the Wendigo or splake). The lamprey would attach itself to the lakers before they had a chance to spawn and suck out their body juices. But a crash program to eliminate the lampreys has shown remarkable results and the lake trout population in the Great Lakes is now slowly on the increase. The flesh of the laker ranges from white to dark pink and can be successfully fried, baked, broiled or smoked.

LAKE TROUT

State or Province	Frequency	Average Size lbs.-ozs.	Record lbs.-ozs.	Year
Alaska	abundant	—	47 – 0	1970
California	present	—	35 – 8	1970
Colorado	abundant	2 – 8	36 – 0	1949
Connecticut	present	—	29 – 13	1918
Idaho	present	—	54 – 5	1964
Illinois	present	4 – 8	—	—
Indiana	present	—	—	—
Maine	abundant	5 – 0	31 – 8	1958
Massachusetts	present	—	13 – 6	1971
Michigan	abundant	6 – 0	53 – 0	1944
Minnesota	abundant	2 – 0	43 – 8	—
Montana	present	—	—	—
Nevada	present	5 – 0	22 – 8	1969
New Hampshire	abundant	4 – 8	28 – 8	1958
New York	abundant	—	31 – 0	1922
Oregon	present	12 – 0	39 – 8	—
Pennsylvania	present	—	24 – 0	1952
Utah	present	8 – 0	—	—
Vermont	present	2 – 0	27 – 8	1971
Virginia	present	—	5 – 6	1966
Washington	present	—	30 – 4	—
Wisconsin	abundant	6 – 0	47 – 0	1946
Wyoming	present	1 – 8	41 – 8	1965
CANADA				
Alberta	present	5 – 0	52 – 8	1928
British Columbia	present	4 – 0	—	—
Manitoba	abundant	—	63 – 0	1930
New Brunswick	abundant	4 – 0	—	—
Newfoundland	abundant	—	—	—

LAKE TROUT (Continued)

State or Province	Frequency	Average Size lbs.-ozs.	Record lbs.-ozs.	Year
N.W. Territories	abundant	5 – 0	65 – 0	1970
Nova Scotia	abundant	4 – 0	—	—
Ontario	abundant	4 – 0	63 – 2	1952
Quebec	abundant	5 – 0	57 – 8	1963
Saskatchewan	abundant	5 – 0	51 – 10	1958
Yukon Territories	abundant	6 – 0	—	—

WENDIGO

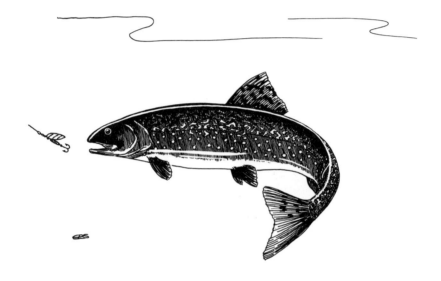

Other names: Splake.

This relatively recent and popular hybrid (*s*peckled trout-*lake* trout) is quickly becoming a must for eastern fishermen.

The name Wendigo is Indian and refers to a spirit that lurks deep in the water. A concerted effort has been made to develop this hybrid both for sport fishing and for food purposes. The combination results in the large size of the lake trout and the game quality and coloring of the speckled trout.

Spawning Habits

The hybrid does spawn, and its habits in this case resemble the brookie. Spawning takes place in early November and the splake prefers gravelly areas where proper protection can be built. The fish spend day and night on the beds borrowing from both antecedents (lakers spawn at night, brookies in the day). The pair defend their spawning areas as do brookies. Incubation is six months.

Appearance

Not unexpectedly, the splake falls between lake trout and brookies in size. The spots on the sides are not as brilliant as those on the brook trout, but much brighter than those on the lake trout, tending to a yellow or pale pink.

Identification can be difficult, particularly when you note that color changes dramatically as does the environment.

One of the major advantages of the Wendigo is that it will help replace the lake trout decimated by lampreys in Lake Huron. Because it spawns at least once before becoming the target of the lamprey, the stock is continued.

Angling Tips

The Wendigo or splake combines the doggedness of the lake trout with the speed and surface gyrations of the brook trout. They are caught during the warm summer months when they will readily rise to the fly.

The Wendigo tends to move in schools so that you might fish unsuccessfully for a long while before making several exciting strikes. Trolling is also a useful technique with the standard range of spinners and spoons. Research has shown they tend to frequent depths around 20 to 35 feet in temperatures of 50 to 70 degrees. And luckily for the angler, the Wendigo takes the bait more easily than either of its half-parents. The three-year old Wendigo averages between 18 and 20 inches in length and 2 pounds in weight. It's too early in this hybrid's career to talk of records, but the largest known catch was a 16 pound Wendigo in 1968. Scientists believe there must be a certain number of 20 pounders in Lake Huron by this time.

WENDIGO

State or Province	Frequency	Average Size lbs.-ozs.	Record lbs.-ozs.	Year
California	present	—	—	—
Colorado	present	1 – 0	6 – 12	1967
Connecticut	present	0 – 12	—	—
Michigan	abundant	—	7 – 8	1968
Minnesota	present	—	—	—
New Hampshire	present	1 – 0	8 – 8	1963
New York	present	—	—	—
Wisconsin	present	—	14 – 4	1967
Wyoming	present	—	—	—

State or Province	Frequency	Average Size lbs.-ozs.	Record lbs.-ozs.	Year
CANADA				
Manitoba .... present		—	7 – 0	1967
Ontario .... present		2 – 0	—	—
Quebec .... present		2 – 0	—	—
Saskatchewan .... present		1 – 8	—	—

ARCTIC CHAR

Other names: Alpine char, sea trout, Hudson's Bay salmon. Subspecies include the Dolly Varden, the red trout, the bull trout, blueback trout and sunapee trout.

Like the Arctic Grayling, the Arctic char is essentially a northern fish being found across the top of Canada from the Yukon to Newfoundland. There are both sea-going and landlocked char, each with its own coloration.

Spawning Habits

The char spawns in October in gravel or sandy beds anywhere up to 18 feet deep. The sea-going variety often linger around the mouths of rivers before making the run inland to spawn, an event which takes place in their fifth year. They feed heavily before going upstream and run in schools.

Appearance

The char is quite a colorful fish, varying widely according to the water conditions. The back ranges from blue to green to brown while the sides can be bright orange or red. In any of these cases, the lateral line cleaves a distinct color bar along the fish. It has been equated to the brook trout in general appearance. The dark fins sometimes are trimmed in white or light colors.

Angling Tips

Fly fishing or spinning are the best methods for Arctic char, and care must be taken to hit the run at the right time or spend hours and days contemplating only the beauties of the north.

The sea-going char travel in schools and the best place to look for them is in shallow, fast-running waters or at river mouths. You will find this fish may stalk your fly for what seems an unbearable length of time before taking it. After taking the hook, this battler may run for 60 feet before leaping into the air to wrest free. It puts up a good fight before tiring. After a long run inland to spawn the fish tend to deteriorate in quality and fighting spirit. For the avid spin casting angler any bright lure will do the trick, but the lighter the lure, the better will be the fight.

The Arctic char makes excellent eating and it has now attained status, having been adopted by Canadians as a dish for state occasions.

ARCTIC CHAR

State or Province	Frequency	Average Size lbs.-ozs.	Record lbs.-ozs.	Year
Alaska	abundant	—	17 – 8	1968
CANADA				
Manitoba	present	—	6 – 0	1961
Newfoundland	abundant	3 – 0	—	—
N.W. Territories	abundant	7 – 8	29 – 11	1968
Quebec	abundant	3 – 0	—	—
Yukon Territories	abundant	—	—	—

DOLLY VARDEN AND RED TROUT

The Dolly Varden in the west and the Quebec red trout in the east are subspecies of the Arctic char.

The Dolly Varden will take any kind of lure and is a cinch for wet or dry flies. It fights vigorously but without style. In appearance it offers a green or brown body covered with red and orange spots on the sides. The sea-going variety appear more silvery. It is a predator which accounts for the mixed feelings it raises in conservationist anglers.

DOLLY VARDEN

State or Province	Frequency	Average Size lbs.-ozs.	Record lbs.-ozs.	Year
California	present	1 – 8	9 – 1	1968
Colorado	present	0 – 8	—	—
Idaho	present	—	32 – 0	1949
Montana	present	—	—	—
Nevada	present	—	—	—
New Mexico	present	—	—	—
Oregon	present	0 – 8	20 – 0	—
Washington	present	—	22 – 8	—

CANADA

Alberta	present	3 – 0	14 – 13	1969
British Columbia	abundant	2 – 8	—	—
N.W. Territories	present	—	—	—
Yukon Territories	abundant	—	—	—

RED TROUT

Province	Frequency	Average Size lbs.-ozs.	Record lbs.-ozs.	Year
Quebec	present	—	3 – 0	—

BLUEBACK TROUT

State	Frequency	Average Size lbs.-ozs.	Record lbs.-ozs.	Year
Maine	present	—	—	—

SUNAPEE TROUT

State	Frequency	Average Size lbs.-ozs.	Record lbs.-ozs.	Year
Maine	present	2 – 0	—	—
New Hampshire	present	4 – 8	11 – 8	1954

Group Three

PACIFIC SALMON

The third major division of the salmon family — the Pacific salmon — is less widely dispersed across North America as the name so aptly suggests. The commercial value of some Pacific salmon far outweighs their contribution to sport fishing and, indeed, some subspecies provide little enjoyment whatsoever. Nonetheless the major Pacific salmons provide fabulous fishing in the north west U.S. and British Columbia. Some species have been successfully transplanted easterly, notably the coho, but for the most part, the Pacific salmon are concentrated just as the name implies.

The five species, sockeye, chum, coho, pink and chinook, run to some 1,500 rivers in Washington, Oregon, Alaska and British Columbia.

CHINOOK SALMON

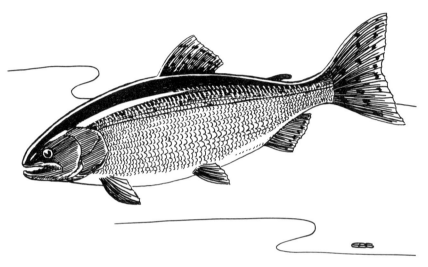

Other names, tyee, king, spring, quinnat.

This most widespread and exciting of the Pacific salmon family ranges from the Northern China coast to central California and the Pacific northwest. Many attempts to transplant the Chinook in the Eastern United States and Canada have only had limited success.

Spawning Habits

After a tenacious fight upstream, past natural and man-made hazards, the 4 or 5 year old Chinook will seek out the gravelly riverbeds from whence it came, to spawn a new generation. The trip from the sea, getting more difficult as man harnesses the waters, can take the Chinook many miles inland. And after the spawning act, this noble fish dies. Two months later, the new arrivals hatch, and after another three months in fresh water, make their way to the sea.

Appearance

The back of the Chinook salmon is greenish, fading to silver on the sides and belly. The back can become almost black, especially during spawning. Above the lateral line will appear many black spots of different sizes. In contradistinction to the brook trout of eastern Canada and others, the Chinook becomes least colorful during spawning which occurs from June to November. Before spawning in their fifth year, this fish weighs up to 50 pounds.

Angling Tips

The Chinook has a fearsome reputation as a fighter, and by one of those illogical quirks which dominate the art of fishing, is called a tyee when it exceeds 30 pounds.

Experts around the world will know that a way of life centered around the catching of the tyee has developed on the continent's west coast.

Catching it is difficult and therefore extra rewarding. One has the entire comercial fishing industry of the Pacific northwest to compete with. One successful method is deep trolling with all the heavy tackle indicated by the weight of the fish. July, August and September are the best months for fishing, with most records being established in the first two weeks of August. These adversaries can also be taken by bait casting and spinning, but fully three-quarters of the sport fishing take is by trolling or chumming.

CHINOOK SALMON

State or Province	Frequency	Average Size lbs.-ozs.	Record lbs.-ozs.	Year
Alaska	abundant	40 – 0	87 – 0	1971
California	abundant	15 – 0	85 – 0	1935
Idaho	present	—	45 – 0	1964
Illinois	present	2 – 0	24 – 0	1970
Indiana	present	—	13 – 14	1970
Michigan	abundant	20 – 0	42 – 0	1970
New York	present	—	—	—
Ohio	present	8 – 0	—	—
Oregon	abundant	18 – 0	83 – 0	—
Washington	abundant	—	70 – 8	1964
Wisconsin	present	10 – 0	35 – 0	1971
CANADA				
British Columbia	abundant	15 – 0	92 – 0	1959
Ontario	present	—	—	—
Yukon Territories	abundant	—	—	—

COHO SALMON

Other names, Sea trout, silver salmon.

The most popular Pacific salmon after the Chinook, this plucky fighter does its battle closer to the surface than its cousin and hence the angler gains a measure of visual enjoyment as it breaks surface, thrashing, twisting, lunging for freedom.

Spawning Habits

The coho populates the fresh water streams closer to the sea than the chinook. In their third or fourth year, they return from the sea and attempt to find their own place of birth. The run may take from August to the following February. At the spawning grounds, the fish pair off and in a depression made by the female the eggs are laid and fertilized. Shortly after, both die. Their fry's first year is spent in fresh or brackish water before moving out to sea.

Appearance

The coho has a longer and more slender body than the chinook with needle-like teeth in its conical head. Many irregularly-placed dark and black spots cover the body. The background color is silvery blue fading off to silver. During the run to spawn, the color changes dramatically, with the background color changing to a lacklustre brown or red. The male develops a hooked snout with heavy dangerous-looking teeth.

Angling Tips

There are many ways to land this fierce, fighting beauty. Here's a tip from a veteran British Columbia angler who refuses to troll for them: "Fish cohos 20-30 feet below the surface using a live herring hooked through the lips and back with No. 6 trebles tied 3 inches apart. A 2-ounce sinker is attached to the line about a yard above the bait." This technique is called mooching. More standard methods are trolling, spinning and fly-casting in both salt and fresh water. Look for flocks of gulls just an hour before or after tide changes. That's when the coho comes to the surface to feed, and when trolling is most effective. In the streams and rivers inland, use your spinning gear with spoons or spinners as the lure.

COHO SALMON

State or Province	Frequency	Average Size lbs.-ozs.	Record lbs.-ozs.	Year
Alaska	abundant	—	21 – 8	1968
Arizona	present	—	—	—
California	present	8 – 0	22 – 0	1959
Illinois	present	—	18 – 0	1970
Indiana	present	—	—	—
Maine	present	5 – 0	—	—
Massachusetts	present	—	—	—
Michigan	abundant	11 – 0	27 – 12	1970
Minnesota	present	2 – 8	10 – 6½	1970
Nebraska	present	—	4 – 4	1970
New Hampshire	present	7 – 0	12 – 9	1970
New York	present	—	—	—
Oregon	abundant	8 – 0	21 – 0	—
Pennsylvania	abundant	—	—	—
Virginia	present	—	8 – 1	1971
Washington	abundant	—	26 – 0	1970
Wisconsin	present	—	19 – 12½	1969

CANADA

British Columbia	abundant	6 – 0	31 – 0	1947
Ontario	abundant	4 – 0	22 – 1	1971
Saskatchewan	present	—	—	—

KOKANEE SALMON

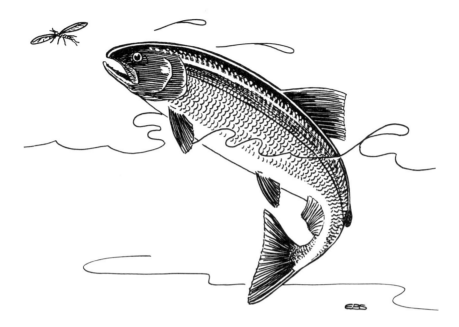

Other names: Kennerly's salmon, silver salmon, red salmon, walla, sockeye, redfish, and blueback.

The kokanee is a smaller landlocked version of the sockeye salmon and while native to the Pacific Northwest, has been successfully transplanted in many places across the continent including New York, Pennsylvania, and Ontario. It is noted both as a sport fish and for its excellent taste on the table.

Appearance

The kokanee has silvery sides with a thin lateral line and a few small spots starting just ahead of the dorsal fin and carrying back to the large and slightly forked tail. They have more than 12 rays in the anal fin.

Spawning Habits

The male develops a hooked lower jaw and the sides become reddish. In the female the silver darkens to grey. The female makes the redd in lakes or streams and, accompanied by the male, moves upstream laying eggs in a sequence of redds. This takes place anytime between late August and January. The male chases away predators. After spawning, both male and female die.

Angling Tips

Trolling perhaps brings the best results for this fierce fighter. The fly-caster will waste hours with his selection of wets and drys for a kokanee to take the bait. Better still-fish or troll with natural bait of corn or worms, and even maggots. If trolling, you'll have to experiment with the depth, but once you find it, stay with it. Only when the kokanee seeks food on the surface does the fly fisherman have a chance. It has a tender mouth, so when trolling fix the hook carefully before playing the fish.

KOKANEE SALMON

State or Province	Frequency	Average Size lbs.-ozs.	Record lbs.-ozs.	Year
Arizona	present	—	—	—
California	present	1 – 12	4 – 4	1967
Colorado	abundant	1 – 4	3 – 0	1963
Connecticut	abundant	1 – 4	—	—
Idaho	present	—	3 – 10	1958
Massachusetts	present	—	—	—
Michigan	present	—	—	—
Missouri	present	0 – 8	—	—
Montana	present	—	—	—
Nebraska	present	—	3 – 12	1970
Nevada	present	1 – 0	—	—
New Mexico	present	1 – 8	—	—
New York	present	—	—	—
North Dakota	present	—	—	—
Oregon	abundant	0 – 12	—	—
Pennsylvania	present	—	—	—
South Dakota	present	—	0 – 12	—
Tennessee	present	0 – 4	—	—
Utah	present	0 – 12	—	—
CANADA				
British Columbia	abundant	1 – 0	8 – 0	—
Ontario	present	1 – 8	—	—
Saskatchewan	present	1 – 8	—	—
Yukon Territories	present	—	—	—

SOCKEYE SALMON

While of enormous value to the west coast commercial fishing industry, the sockeye is of little value to the angler, disdaining as he does the bait or lure.

PINK SALMON

Its other name, Humpback, was acquired because during spawning it develops a noticeable hump behind the head and a menacing hooked upper jaw.

The pink salmon is the smallest of the Pacific salmon, and while of great importance commercially is nonetheless a good game fish for the angler. Superimposed on its slate-blue back are many irregular black spots of differing shapes. The sides become silvery in color, sliding off to white on the belly. During spawning, the black spots diffuse and tend to melt in with the general overall color.

A good pink will weigh anywhere from 6 to 12 pounds and can be caught along the coast of the Pacific northwest. It doesn't migrate as far inland as the other varieties, making the coastal fishing most rewarding. Trolling, spinning and strip casting work well in the salt water areas. Small inland populations exist.

CHUM SALMON

Other name, Dog salmon, because of the heavy teeth and the hooked jaws which develop when it enters fresh water.

The chum is the least attractive of the Pacific salmon family, partly because the taste does not approach the others, and partly because it doesn't take to the lure frequently enough to attract the angler. When hooked, it can put up a good fight, but generally anglers try for the more venturesome and flavorsome varieties. As a commercial fish, however, it is extremely popular. When it is in its visual prime, in salt water, it has a slate-blue back with the occasional series of spots. The fins, however, are frequently tinged with black.

LARGEMOUTH BASS

Other names: Big-mouthed bass, linesides, green bass, green trout, lake bass, mossback, and northern largemouth bass.

The largemouth bass and the smallmouth bass (which follows) are not really bass at all, a fact which will be of extreme irrelevance to the thousands of avid large-and-smallmouth fishermen. They are of the sunfish family, which also includes the rock bass and black and white crappies.

Spawning Habits

Sometime in the spring, the male of the species builds the nest in quiet areas of lakes and rivers seeking gravelly, clay or mud bottoms. The male and female simultaneously emit eggs and milt resulting in fertilization. After this act, the female departs, leaving the male to fend off attackers and fan the nest with his fins. The eggs hatch in about 10 days, less if the water is warm, and the male continues his parental chores until the fry are about an inch long. The male will strike at a lure readily when watching over the redd but is usually out of season at that point.

Appearance

The major distinguishing feature between the large and small-mouth bass, aside from size, is that the upper jaw of the largemouth extends past the eye, while in the smallmouth, the jaw ends directly beneath the eye.

The largemouth bass varies in color from location to location but generally speaking, it has a dark green back fading to a greenish-silver color on the sides fading to white on the belly. There is a large band of dark spots which run from the gills to the tail, and the dorsal fin is deeply notched, with 9 or 10 spines ahead of 12 to 13 soft rays. The eye is golden or amber, and the clearer the water, the more distinct the markings.

Angling Tips

The supreme attraction of the bigmouth for the less active fisherman is that it likes warmer water and will hit almost anything the angler cares to introduce into the water. It hits poppers, bugs, chuggers, spoons, spinners, jigs, plastic and rubber worms, eels, and other imitations. In fact there are probably more bass lures produced than for any other kind of fish.

112

The largemouth favors waters covered with heavy vegetation but does not restrict itself solely to these locales.

Look for shallow, mud-bottomed-lakes and slow-moving streams which have an abundance of plant life. As the summer advances, old mossback tends to head for deeper waters although still favoring the weed-festooned locales. All those stumps, rocks, piers, overhangs, rocky ledges and sunken logs as well as all weedy patches can harbor the largemouth.

Shallow waters are usual feeding grounds and the largemouth will defend a good spot from all comers. Generally they'll feed on worms, mussels, frogs, crayfish, water snakes, other fish including their own kind and all available insects. They feed most actively in the morning and evening at the surface, moving deeper during the heat of the day.

This quarry will strike a variety of lures and bait and put up a good fight when hooked.

Don't forget that while the bigmouth may appear to snap at anything, it may be from anger rather than hunger, and they can become extremely wary in well-fished waters.

Once hooked, one of the more exciting moments occurs when he appears to stand on his tail and waves his head back and forth trying to shake the hook.

Take a wide assortment of lures when you go bass fishing. The variety of places the largemouth might be, coupled with its wariness, will take a good sampling of your tackle box. In fact you can keep changing the lure until you find one that will intrigue or aggravate the fish into striking.

Be careful when approaching your proposed fishing area not to upset the environment by careening in at 30 knots, thereby sending your quarry off to quieter climes.

Begin with surface plugs, especially in the early morning or evening, in shallow waters. If they fail, then move on to shallow-running underwater plugs, and if they fail then go to the deep sinking lures in the deeper locations. When casting fails, trolling in deeper water is advised. Spoons, spinners, and minnows should be trolled at various depths, closer to the shore in the morning and toward the deeper parts in mid-day. If you're using live bait, such as frogs, minnows or worms, let the largemouth swallow the bait before setting the hook.

LARGEMOUTH BASS

State or Province	Frequency	Average Size lbs.-ozs.	Record lbs.-ozs.	Year
Alabama	abundant	1 – 0	13 – 12	1969
Arizona	abundant	2 – 0	14 – 10	1966
Arkansas	abundant	1 – 8	12 – 1	1961
California	abundant	3 – 0	16 – 11	1971
Colorado	present	3 – 0	9 – 0	1964
Connecticut	abundant	2 – 0	12 – 14	1961
Delaware	abundant	1 – 8	8 – 9	1971
Florida	abundant	4 – 0	—	—
Georgia	abundant	3 – 0	22 – 4	1932
Idaho	present	—	10 – 15	—
Illinois	present	1 – 8	12 – 8	1969
Indiana	abundant	—	11 – 11	1968
Iowa	abundant	2 – 0	10 – 5	1970
Kansas	abundant	1 – 8	11 – 3	1965
Kentucky	abundant	3 – 0	13 – 8	1966
Louisiana	abundant	—	11 – 11	1958
Maine	abundant	3 – 8	11 – 10	1968
Maryland	abundant	1 – 0	10 – 1	1966
Massachusetts	abundant	—	12 – 1	1963
Michigan	abundant	1 – 0	11 – 15	1934
Minnesota	abundant	1 – 8	10 – 2	—
Mississippi	abundant	2 – 8	13 – 2	1963
Missouri	abundant	1 – 8	13 – 14	1961
Montana	present	—	—	—
Nebraska	abundant	—	10 – 11	1965
Nevada	present	2 – 8	9 – 13	1968
New Hampshire	abundant	2 – 8	10 – 8	1967
New Jersey	abundant	—	10 – 12	1960
New Mexico	abundant	2 – 0	9 – 8	1971
New York	abundant	—	10 – 6	1931 and 1942
North Carolina	abundant	1 – 8	14 – 15	1963
North Dakota	present	1 – 8	7 – 12	1951
Ohio	abundant	2 – 8	9 – 9	1970
Oklahoma	abundant	2 – 0	11 – 15	1941
Oregon	present	2 – 8	10 – 8	—
Pennsylvania	abundant	—	8 – 8	1936
Rhode Island	abundant	2 – 0	9 – 12	1963
South Carolina	abundant	3 – 0	16 – 2	1949
South Dakota	abundant	1 – 8	8 – 12	—
Tennessee	abundant	1 – 0	14 – 8	1954
Texas	abundant	1 – 4	13 – 8	1943
Utah	present	1 – 0	—	—
Vermont	present	2 – 0	16 – 14	1970
Virginia	abundant	—	13 – 4	1971
Washington	present	2 – 0	11 – 8	1966
West Virginia	abundant	1 – 8	9 – 2	1966
Wisconsin	abundant	2 – 0	11 – 3	1940
Wyoming	present	0 – 12	7 – 2	1942

State or Province	Frequency	Average Size lbs.-ozs.	Record lbs.-ozs.	Year
CANADA				
British Columbia	present	1 – 8	5 – 8	—
Manitoba	present	—	5 – 1	1970
Ontario	abundant	1 – 8	14 – 2	1948
Quebec	present	3 – 0	5 – 15	1957
Saskatchewan	present	1 – 8	—	—

SMALLMOUTH BASS

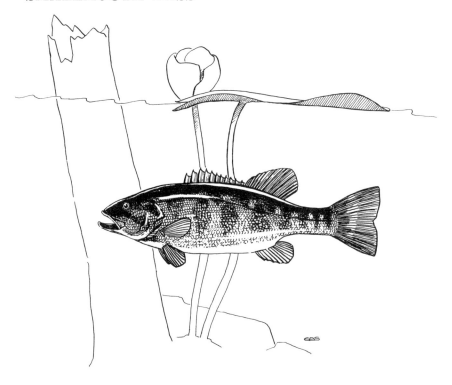

Other names: black perch, brown bass, black bass, river bass, tiger bass, gold bass, redeye bass and bronze back.

This most popular member of the sunfish family has many similar characteristics to the largemouth bass, but is easily distinguishable in two major ways, the back of the jaw is even with the eye and it has longer vertical markings extending from gill to tail.

Spawning Habits

This meticulous creature expends much effort in reproduction. The male seeks out a gravel bed, which it fans clean of all particles until the stones beneath are unencumbered. It may use its nose to push aside troublesome bits of dirt. The nest may be as big as three feet in diameter and a couple of inches deep. The male then solicits the female and the eggs are promptly fertilized. For the next 3 to 12 days the anxious male fends off intruders and fans away silt from the eggs. The spawning season extends from May to July depending on the temperature.

Appearance

The dorsal fin is notched in the same manner as the largemouth bass with stiff spines followed by softer rays on the back. The smallmouth can change color more quickly than most fish but the generally accepted distinguishable coloration is dark green to dark brown fading off to white on the belly. In warmer climates the dark green can appear bronze and the eye a bright red.

Angling Tips

The bronze back is a better fighter than the bigmouth and is considered one of the most vicious of opponents. Once caught however, you'll notice it is clean, pleasing to the eye, and equally pleasing to the palate.

The smallmouth prefers slightly cooler waters to the largemouth, the former gives the angler a better battle for his money.

The smallmouth likes a vigorous life, and seeks out rocky rivers where the current flows clean and fast. You can frequently spot them in pools near the base of a waterfall or rapids, or near boulders where the water plays fast on either side. In lakes, the smallmouth can be found in deeper surroundings, especially along deep rocky shorelines, or around shoals.

The same tackle used to land largemouth bass will do for bronze backs. This fish responds to flies, plugs, spinners, spoons, jigs, frogs, worms, crawfish, minnows or leeches. However, surface plugging for them is not generally productive.

His striking is unpredictable; he may refuse all offerings then suddenly start hitting madly.

SMALLMOUTH BASS

State or Province	Frequency	Average Size lbs.-ozs.	Record lbs.-ozs.	Year
Alabama	present	1 – 0	10 – 8	1950
Arizona	present	0 – 12	4 – 1.5	1969
Arkansas	abundant	0 – 14	7 – 5	1969
California	present	2 – 8	7 – 11	1951

State or Province	Frequency	Average Size lbs.-ozs.	Record lbs.-ozs.	Year
Colorado	present	2 – 0	—	—
Connecticut	abundant	2 – 0	7 – 10	1954
Delaware	present	0 – 12	7 – 0	1971
Georgia	abundant	2 – 0	6 – 5	1969
Idaho	present	—	5 – 14	1962
Illinois	present	1 – 0	5 – 13	1970
Indiana	abundant	—	6 – 8	1970
Iowa	abundant	—	6 – 3	1966
Kansas	present	0 – 12	2 – 7	1971
Kentucky	abundant	1 – 8	11 – 13	1955
Maine	abundant	2 – 0	8 – 0	1970
Maryland	abundant	0 – 12	8 – 0	1968
Massachusetts	abundant	—	6 – 12	1967
Michigan	abundant	0 – 12	9 – 4	1906
Minnesota	abundant	1 – 4	8 – 0	—
Mississippi	present	1 – 8	—	—
Missouri	abundant	1 – 0	6 – 7	1952
Montana	present	—	—	—
Nebraska	present	—	4 – 10	1970
Nevada	present	1 – 0	—	—
New Hampshire	abundant	1 – 8	6 – 0	1969
New Jersey	present	—	6 – 4	1957
New Mexico	present	0 – 12	3 – 4	1970
New York	abundant	—	9 – 0	1925
North Carolina	abundant	1 – 0	10 – 2	1953
North Dakota	present	1 – 0	—	—
Ohio	abundant	2 – 0	7 – 8	1941
Oklahoma	present	0 – 12	4 – 12	1968
Oregon	present	1 – 8	4 – 9	—
Pennsylvania	abundant	—	6 – 2	1937
Rhode Island	present	1 – 8	—	—
South Carolina	present	—	—	—
South Dakota	present	—	1 – 14	—
Tennessee	abundant	0 – 12	11 – 15	1955
Texas	present	2 – 0	—	—
Vermont	present	1 – 8	6 – 7	1969
Virginia	abundant	—	8 – 0	—
Washington	present	1 – 8	7 – 8	1964
West Virginia	abundant	1 – 0	9 – 4	1971
Wisconsin	present	—	9 – 1	1950
Wyoming	present	0 – 8	—	—

CANADA

British Columbia	present	1 – 8	—	—
Manitoba	present	—	6 – 8	1959
New Brunswick	abundant	1 – 8	—	—
Nova Scotia	present	1 – 8	—	—
Ontario	abundant	1 – 8	11 – 6	1960
Quebec	present	2 – 8	8 – 12	1968
Saskatchewan	present	1 – 8	—	—

BLACK CRAPPIE

Other names: Calico bass, strawberry bass, or speckled perch.

The black crappie, and the closely related white crappie, are spread extensively throughout the continent, with the black version being slightly more prevalent. Both are particular favorites in the south and midwest states, but wherever the angler finds them, they provide excellent sport and good eating.

Spawning Habits

Both species are early spawners, ensuring the next generation when temperatures reach about 55 degrees, although the ideal temperature has been pegged at 68 degrees. Depth can range from 10 inches to 10 feet.

Appearance

Crappies can be recognized by their large, rounded dorsal and anal fins and their deep but narrow bodies giving a pancake appearance. The black crappie has seven or eight dorsal spines, and dark, irregularly spaced blotches on the side. The white version has only six dorsal spines and is shaded with a pattern of vertical bars. Not unnaturally, the black crappie is generally darker than the white, although at spawning time confusion can occur. One way to make sure is by examining the lower jaw: In the black it protrudes more noticeably than in the white crappie. Another telltale sign is the eyes; blacks show a deep blue with a gold circle around the iris, the white's eyes are lighter in color.

Angling Tips

The black likes the clear, cool water of gravelly or rock bottomed streams. They are often found congregated around old pilings, snags, or near the mouths of streams. In the summer the crappie stays near the bottom in up to 20 feet of water, in deeper bays and channels. They like to feed in the darker depths, only feeding in shallow water during the early hours or at dusk.

The black crappie is one of the few members of the sunfish family that continues to feed during the winter, and therefore provides excellent fishing during that period.

Good, active shiners between one and two inches serve as best bait for the crappies. A number 6 or 4 short-shanked hook is best and should be fixed either in the tail or through the lips. A small gold spinner just about the bait is useful. Using a float, never, never, never jerk the line when the bait is taken. Allow the fish time to mouth the bait and head for deeper water before setting the hook. That way you'll avoid tearing the tender mouth and losing bait and fish. After a few tugs and a short run or two, it will come to the surface easily.

Look for a cloudy overcast day with high humidity for best results. On clear dry days, the crappie will head for the depths or for cover of some kind.

It takes practice to handle a spinning rod with float and shiner at the action end. Other useful artificial bait includes streamers, spinners, small spoons, small poppers, and high-riding hair bugs.

BLACK CRAPPIE

State or Province	Frequency	Average Size lbs.-ozs.	Record lbs.-ozs.	Year
Alabama	abundant	0 – 8	—	—
Arizona	present	—	4 – 10	1959
Arkansas	abundant	0 – 8	3 – 14	1966
California	abundant	0 – 8	4 – 0	1956
Colorado	abundant	0 – 8	4 – 0	1950
Connecticut	abundant	0 – 10	3 – 13	1955
Delaware	abundant	0 – 8	—	—
Florida	abundant	—	—	—
Georgia	abundant	0 – 12	4 – 4	1971
Illinois	present	0 – 4	4 – 4	1967
Indiana	abundant	—	—	—
Iowa	abundant	—	—	—
Kansas	abundant	0 – 4	4 – 10	1957
Kentucky	abundant	1 – 0	—	—
Louisiana	abundant	0 – 12	—	—
Maine	present	0 – 12	—	—
Maryland	present	—	—	—
Massachusetts	present	—	2 – 9½	1965
Michigan	abundant	—	4 – 2	1947
Minnesota	abundant	—	—	—
Mississippi	abundant	0 – 8	—	—
Missouri	abundant	0 – 8	4 – 8	1967
Montana	present	—	—	—
Nebraska	abundant	—	—	—
Nevada	present	0 – 4	2 – 3	1969
New Jersey	present	—	3 – 5½	1966
New Mexico	present	0 – 4	—	—
New York	abundant	1 – 0	—	—
North Carolina	abundant	0 – 8	—	—
North Dakota	abundant	—	—	—
Ohio	abundant	0 – 6	3 – 8	1968
Oklahoma	abundant	0 – 8	—	—
Oregon	abundant	0 – 8	2 – 6	—
Pennsylvania	abundant	—	—	—
Rhode Island	present	0 – 8	—	—

BLACK CRAPPIE (Continued)

State or Province	Frequency	Average Size lbs.-ozs.	Record lbs.-ozs.	Year
South Carolina	abundant	1 – 0	5 – 0	1957
South Dakota	present	—	3 – 2	—
Tennessee	abundant	0 – 8	2 – 6	1970
Texas	abundant	1 – 0	—	—
Utah	abundant	—	—	—
Vermont	present	—	—	—
Virginia	abundant	—	4 – 13½	1967
Washington	present	—	—	—
West Virginia	abundant	0 – 8	—	—
Wisconsin	abundant	0 – 8	4 – 8	1967
Wyoming	present	0 – 4	—	—
CANADA				
British Columbia	present	0 – 4	—	—
Manitoba	present	—	—	—
Ontario	present	0 – 6	—	—

WHITE CRAPPIE

Other names: white perch, bachelor perch, camplite, lamplighter, paper mouth and, in Louisiana, sac à lait, referring to the white, flaky texture of the flesh.

The white crappie is more at home in turbid waters and mud bottoms than the black crappie. The whites grow a little faster than the black and both species are short-lived, four to six years being the average. While providing as good eating as the black, the white crappie is considered slightly less sportier in the water. Both varieties tend to travel in schools, providing excellent fishing when located.

WHITE CRAPPIES

State	Frequency	Average Size lbs.-ozs.	Record lbs.-ozs.	Year
Alabama	abundant	0 – 8	3 – 12	1971
Arizona	present	—	1 – 11	1971
Arkansas	abundant	0 – 8	4 – 0	1969
California	abundant	0 – 8	4 – 8	1971
Colorado	abundant	0 – 8	—	—
Delaware	abundant	0 – 8	2 – 12	1971
Georgia	abundant	0 – 12	4 – 4	1968
Idaho	present	—	2 – 8	1954
Illinois	present	0 – 4	4 – 5	1967
Indiana	abundant	—	4 – 7	1965
Iowa	abundant	—	4 – 1	1966
Kansas	abundant	0 – 4	4 – 0¼	1964
Kentucky	abundant	1 – 0	4 – 0	1971

State	Frequency	Average Size lbs.-ozs.	Record lbs.-ozs.	Year
Louisiana	abundant	0 – 12	6 – 0	1969
Maryland	present	0 – 4	3 – 4	1968
Massachusetts	present	—	—	—
Michigan	present	—	—	—
Minnesota	abundant	0 – 5	5 – 0	—
Mississippi	abundant	0 – 12	5 – 3	—
Missouri	abundant	0 – 12	3 – 12	1964
Montana	present	—	—	—
Nebraska	abundant	—	3 – 15	1962
Nevada	present	0 – 4	2 – 8	1968
New Mexico	abundant	0 – 4	—	—
New York	abundant	1 – 0	—	—
North Carolina	abundant	0 – 8	4 – 8	1960
North Dakota	abundant	2 – 0	3 – 0	1958
Ohio	abundant	0 – 6	3 – 5	1968
Oklahoma	abundant	0 – 8	4 – 13	1967
Oregon	abundant	0 – 8	2 – 1	—
Pennsylvania	abundant	—	3 – 8	—
South Carolina	abundant	1 – 0	5 – 1	1949
South Dakota	abundant	—	2 – 11	—
Tennessee	abundant	0 – 8	5 – 1	1968
Texas	abundant	1 – 0	4 – 3	1967
Utah	present	—	—	—
Virginia	abundant	—	—	—
Washington	present	—	4 – 8	1956
West Virginia	abundant	0 – 8	4 – 0	—
Wisconsin	abundant	0 – 3	—	—

WALLEYE

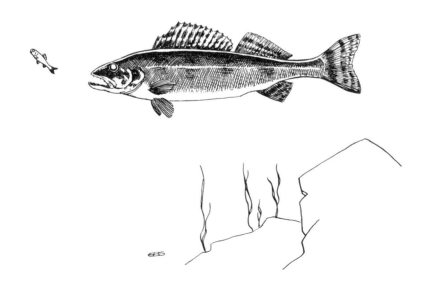

Other names: (a veritable landslide) Dore (in Quebec), pike-perch, walleyed pike, yellow pikeperch, yellow pike, yellow pickerel. Jack salmon, golden pike, and opal eye. This large diversity of names is unfortunate in that it confuses the walleye of the perch family with at least two other major species, the pike family and the trout family. It is of the perch family, and its proper name is walleye.

This is a most entertaining fish, being spread extensively over the continent, at once, difficult to find, and easy to land once hooked.

They travel in schools, way beneath the surface. But, when you get the lure close enough, the creature will obligingly strike, retreat to sulk, and come to its end with little panoply. The secret here is to find a school, and fish like hell.

Apart from sport fishing, the walleye is a popular commercial fish, but such are its reproductive habits that there appears to be no danger of depleting the supply.

Spawning Habits

The walleye spawns in the spring. The fish seeks out fast rivers, males first, and eggs and milt are emitted simultaneously into the water where they match up and then stick to the bottom. Two or three weeks later, the eggs hatch and the young venture forth.

Appearance

The walleye, true to its name, has large, glassy eyes. It has an elongated head, a cylindrical body upon which is mounted two separate dorsal fins, the first spiny, the second soft-rayed. The jaws contain tearing teeth which immediately suggest you use wire leader when angling.

Its coloration is olive to dark brown with a yellow mottling effect. The fins tend to be yellowish or pinkish, and if you examine the lower portion of the tail fin closely you will find a white margin as if to say 'This is the end.'

Angling Tips

The walleye prefers the cooler lakes and rivers. Angling is most productive in the early spring and late fall, when day-long fishing is in order. During the warmer months, fish deep, the best times being morning and evening.

The walleye travel in schools, which explains the difficulty in locating them. When you do get a bite, and it can be a vicious one, mark the area so you can keep trying for more. In the spring when they are looking for spawning grounds, it's easier to track them down. They tend to feed close to shore and a school of minnows can lead you to a hungrier school of walleye. In the deeper lakes, slow trolling systematically covering the area is the only way to find your school. Starting at the shore and working outward and downward is the best approach.

Almost any lure will attract a walleye, spoons, spinner combinations, plugs, minnows etc. If you use live bait, give the walleye a chance to swallow it before setting the hook. It takes him some time to accomplish this feat. After that one brief thrill when he takes the lure, the rest is just careful hard work to bring him slowly to the surface without breaking the line.

During the winter months the walleye continues to feed and hence is good for ice fishing.

WALLEYE

State or Province	Frequency	Average Size lbs.-ozs.	Record lbs.-ozs.	Year
Alabama	present	1 – 8	8 – 4	1970
Arizona	present	—	5 – 3	1970
Arkansas	abundant	3 – 0	19 – 12	1963
California	present	—	—	—
Colorado	abundant	2 – 8	16 – 0	1960
Connecticut	present	2 – 0	14 – 8	1941
Georgia	abundant	—	11 – 0	1963
Illinois	present	3 – 0	14 – 0	1961
Indiana	present	—	13 – 0	1969
Iowa	abundant	—	—	—
Kansas	present	2 – 0	12 – 3½	1971
Kentucky	present	6 – 0	21 – 8	1958
Louisiana	present	—	—	—
Maryland	present	3 – 0	8 – 12	1970
Massachusetts	present	—	13 – 8	1971
Michigan	abundant	1 – 8	17 – 3	1951
Minnesota	abundant	1 – 5	16 – 11	—
Missouri	present	2 – 8	20 – 0	1961
Montana	present	—	—	—
Nebraska	abundant	—	16 – 1	1959
Nevada	present	—	—	—
New Hampshire	present	3 – 0	—	—
New Jersey	present	—	12 – 12¾	1934
New Mexico	abundant	3 – 0	8 – 10	1971
New York	abundant	—	15 – 3	1952
North Carolina	abundant	1 – 0	13 – 4	1966
North Dakota	abundant	1 – 8	15 – 12	1959

WALLEYE (Continued)

State or Province	Frequency	Average Size lbs.-ozs.	Record lbs.-ozs.	Year
Ohio	abundant	2 – 0	15 – 0	1951
Oklahoma	present	1 – 0	—	—
Pennsylvania	abundant	2 – 0	12 – 0	1951
South Carolina	present	3 – 0	—	—
South Dakota	abundant	—	15 – 0	—
Tennessee	abundant	1 – 8	25 – 0	1960
Texas	present	1 – 8	—	—
Utah	present	1 – 0	—	—
Vermont	present	2 – 0	10 – 7	1970
Virginia	abundant	—	17 – 0	1965
Washington	present	—	10 – 0	1965
West Virginia	present	1 – 8	16 – 2	1967
Wisconsin	abundant	2 – 0	18 – 0	1933
Wyoming	present	—	9 – 2	1964
CANADA				
Alberta	abundant	2 – 8	14 – 0	1960
British Columbia	present	—	—	—
Manitoba	abundant	—	18 – 8	1954
N.W. Territories	present	2 – 8	—	—
Ontario	abundant	3 – 0	22 – 8	—
Quebec	present	3 – 0	20 – 2	1964
Saskatchewan	abundant	2 – 0	13 – 9	1953

SAUGER

Other names: Eastern sauger, sand pickerel, sand pike, river pike, spotfin pike and jack salmon.

The sauger is a close relative of the walleye, and exhibits many of the same characteristics. There is a definite tendency for this fish to prosper only in large bodies of water, large lakes or rivers.

Appearance

This beauty is long and slender, and has spines on its first dorsal fin. The 3 rows of dark spots on this dorsal fin help distinguish it from the walleye. The back is grey or brown in color shading down to a white belly. There are a number of large splotches on the flank which form a regular pattern. The jaws have sharp, tough teeth. There are dark brown vertical bars on the tail fin.

Spawning Habits

Virtually identical to the walleye.

Angling Tips

The sauger is becoming more approachable as the mid- and southwest burgeon with large dams. It runs in the late fall and can

124

often be found at the tailwaters of power dams. See the walleye chapter for further angling tips.

SAUGER

State or Province	Frequency	Average Size lbs.-ozs.	Record lbs.-ozs.	Year
Alabama	present	0 – 12	—	—
Arkansas	abundant	0 – 12	3 – 15	1967
Illinois	present	1 – 0	5 – 12½	1967
Indiana	abundant	—	5 – 0	1964
Iowa	abundant	—	5 – 2	1963
Kansas	present	0 – 8	—	—
Kentucky	abundant	—	4 – 1	1968
Louisiana	present	—	—	—
Michigan	present	—	3 – 9	1963
Minnesota	present	1 – 0	6 – 2½	—
Mississippi	present	1 – 8	—	—
Missouri	present	—	—	—
Montana	present	—	—	—
Nebraska	present	—	8 – 5	1961
New York	present	—	—	—
North Carolina	present	—	—	—
North Dakota	abundant	—	8 – 6	1971
Ohio	present	1 – 8	—	—
Oklahoma	present	0 – 8	—	—
Oregon	present	—	—	—
Pennsylvania	present	—	—	—
South Dakota	present	—	7 – 7	—
Vermont	present	1 – 8	—	—
West Virginia	present	0 – 8	1 – 4	1971
Wisconsin	abundant	1 – 0	4 – 5	1970
Wyoming	present	1 – 8	6 – 8	1971

CANADA

State or Province	Frequency	Average Size lbs.-ozs.	Record lbs.-ozs.	Year
Alberta	present	—	—	—
Manitoba	abundant	—	3 – 2	1959
Ontario	present	0 – 8	—	—
Saskatchewan	abundant	1 – 0	—	—

YELLOW PERCH

Other names: Red perch, raccoon perch, ringed perch, lake perch, American perch, English perch, zebra or striped perch.

The most important thing to say about a yellow perch is that it's about the most widely caught fish in North America, and a large number of the successful anglers are young children. This saucy little item is not only delicious but also prolific and easy to catch, a good fish to start the children on because the disappointments are fewer.

It is not considered a game fish, but is so popular that its omission would be unfair to its many advocates.

Like other and larger members of the perch family, the yellow perch has the double dorsal fin, spiny in front, ray-like at the rear, with a clear series of dark vertical bars that run along the yellow sides. Its jaws contain sharp teeth, and is compressed, a fact which does not indicate undernourishment.

The yellow perch is an easy fish to catch, especially if you know a few simple facts about its movements. It runs up creeks, rivers and shallow bays to spawn during the spring, leaving its eggs wrapped in a gelatinous film to drift as they might. There is no special time of the day or year to catch them, for even ice fishermen reel in huge quantities during the winter. They tend to wander in schools, but this doesn't preclude finding them in a random manner. As with many other fish, they like to go deeper during the hot summer months, but careful trolling or drifting will reveal a school. While you can fish for yellow perch with almost any of the sophisticated equipment, good old-fashioned still-fishing is successful.

Anywhere along the river or lake bank, near stone pilings or wharfs, near drop-offs or reed beds, on the lee side of points, in fact almost anywhere is good perch country.

And while most of the smaller lures are successful, most yellow perch are taken with live bait, minnows or worms beings the most popular.

During the winter, ice fishermen take scores of yellow perch using tiny live or salted minnows, barley, cheese, tapioca and the like.

The yellow perch is not the toughest fighter in the water, and properly hooked puts up only token resistance before coming in for the coup.

YELLOW PERCH

State or Province	Frequency	Average Size lbs.-ozs.	Record lbs.-ozs.	Year
Alabama	present	0 – 4	—	—
Arizona	present	—	—	—
California	present	0 – 8	—	—
Colorado	abundant	0 – 6	1 – 8	1954
Connecticut	abundant	⇀ 0 – 10	2 – 2	1967
Georgia	abundant	0 – 4	—	—
Idaho	present	—	2 – 8	—
Illinois	present	0 – 4	2 – 5	1951
Indiana	abundant	—	1 – 11	1966
Iowa	abundant	—	1 – 13	1963
Kansas	present	0 – 4	0 – 12	1970
Maine	abundant	0 – 6	—	—
Maryland	present	—	1 – 12	1964
Massachusetts	abundant	—	2 – 5	1970
Michigan	abundant	0 – 4	3 – 12	1947
Minnesota	abundant	0 – 4	3 – 4	—
Montana	abundant	—	—	—
Nebraska	abundant	—	2 – 0	1966
Nevada	present	0 – 2	—	—
New Hampshire	abundant	0 – 2	—	—
New Jersey	present	—	4 – 3½	1865
New Mexico	present	0 – 4	1 – 4	1971
New York	abundant	—	—	—
North Carolina	abundant	0 – 8	—	—
North Dakota	abundant	0 – 8	2 – 2	1966
Ohio	abundant	0 – 4	2 – 8	1954
Oregon	present	0 – 5	1 – 6	—
Pennsylvania	abundant	—	18″	1936
Rhode Island	abundant	0 – 8	—	—
South Carolina	present	0 – 8	—	—
South Dakota	abundant	—	2 – 3	—
Tennessee	present	0 – 3	—	—
Texas	present	0 – 4	—	—
Utah	present	0 – 4	—	—
Vermont	abundant	0 – 4	—	—
Virginia	present	—	1 – 12	1971
West Virginia	present	0 – 4	1 – 0	1971
Wisconsin	present	0 – 4	3 – 4	1954
Wyoming	present	0 – 2	—	—
CANADA				
Alberta	abundant	0 – 12	2 – 4	1967
British Columbia	present	1 – 0	—	—
Manitoba	abundant	—	2 – 5	1970
New Brunswick	abundant	0 – 4	—	—

YELLOW PERCH (Continued)

State or Province	Frequency	Average Size lbs.-ozs.	Record lbs.-ozs.	Year
Newfoundland	present	0 – 8	—	—
N.W. Territories	present	—	—	—
Nova Scotia	abundant	0 – 4	—	—
Ontario	abundant	0 – 8	—	—
Quebec	present	0 – 12	4 – 1	1957
Saskatchewan	abundant	0 – 8	2 – 7	1953

BLUEGILL SUNFISH

Other names: Bream, sunperch, copperbelly, sunfish, roach, blue sunfish.

Appearance

This ever popular panfish is only occasionally blue; it varies in color from virtual transparency to dark blue to yellow, depending on its frequent habitat. Three spines preceed the soft rays in the anal fin, and there are a series of oblong spots or blotches on the last few soft rays of the dorsal fin. A series of vertical bars on the sides gives this fish a distinctive appearance.

Spawning Habits

The bluegill starts spawning in the spring and continues until August, depending on temperature. Shallow nests are created, and after the female emits her eggs, the male stands guard over the gravelly or sandy nest. The young grow about an inch or so a year.

Angling Tips

Wet and dry flies, artificial lures, night crawlers, in fact almost anything will tempt this small but tasty tidbit. Once hooked, it puts up a short but vigorous fight, and the angler who takes it with light spinning gear will have a moment of pleasure.

BLUEGILL SUNFISH

State or Province	Frequency	Average Size lbs.-ozs.	Record lbs.-ozs.	Year
Alabama	abundant	0 – 4	4 – 12	1950
Arizona	abundant	—	3 – 5	1965
Arkansas	abundant	0 – 6	—	—
California	abundant	—	2 – 9	1971
Colorado	present	0 – 4	—	—
Connecticut	abundant	0 – 8	1 – 12	1970
Delaware	abundant	0 – 8	1 – 4	1971
Florida	abundant	—	—	—
Georgia	abundant	0 – 8	2 – 15½	1965

State or Province	Frequency	Average Size lbs.-ozs.	Record lbs.-ozs.	Year
Idaho	present	—	3 – 8	1966
Illinois	present	0 – 4	2 – 10	1963
Indiana	abundant	—	2 – 12	1965
Iowa	abundant	—	2 – 3	1971
Kansas	abundant	0 – 3	2 – 5	1962
Kentucky	abundant	0 – 4	3 – 6	—
Louisiana	abundant	0 – 5	—	—
Maryland	abundant	0 – 4	1 – 14	1970
Massachusetts	abundant	—	1 – 0	1965
Michigan	abundant	0 – 8	2 – 10	1945
Minnesota	abundant	0 – 4	2 – 13	—
Mississippi	abundant	0 – 5	2 – 5	1963
Missouri	abundant	0 – 6	3 – 0	—
Montana	present	—	—	—
Nebraska	abundant	—	2 – 8	1968
Nevada	present	—	—	—
New Hampshire	present	0 – 5	—	—
New Jersey	abundant	—	2 – 0	1956
New Mexico	abundant	0 – 3	1 – 1	1971
New York	abundant	—	—	—
North Carolina	abundant	0 – 6	4 – 5	1967
North Dakota	abundant	0 – 4	2 – 12	—
Ohio	abundant	0 – 4	—	—
Oklahoma	abundant	0 – 1.6	1 – 7	1968
Oregon	abundant	0 – 4	1 – 14	—
Pennsylvania	abundant	—	12½ "	1965
Rhode Island	abundant	0 – 8	—	—
South Carolina	abundant	—	2 – 8	—
South Dakota	abundant	—	2 – 1	—
Tennessee	abundant	0 – 5	2 – 8	1956 and 1961
Texas	abundant	0 – 2	3 – 4	1966
Utah	present	—	—	—
Vermont	present	—	—	—
Virginia	abundant	—	4 – 8	1970
Washington	present	—	—	—
West Virginia	abundant	0 – 4	2 – 2	1964
Wisconsin	abundant	0 – 4	2 – 4	1971
Wyoming	present	0 – 2	—	—
CANADA				
British Columbia	present	0 – 4	—	—

REDEAR SUNFISH

Other names: Shellcracker, bream, yellow bream or stump-knocker.

Appearance

This excellent panfish, common in the south and now being

transplanted westwards, has a red tip on the lobe of the gill covers (red on the males, more orange on females) leading quite naturally to its most common name. Look for the dark vertical bars on the side, against a background of olive and deeper olive spots. There are no spots on the dorsal fin, a fact which should help the angler distinguish it from the pumpkinseed, its closest relative.

Spawning Habits

Spawning takes place in late spring and early summer, while the incubation takes anywhere from five days to two weeks. Like all other sunfish, the male constructs the nest in one to three feet of water, and uses his tail as a whisk to clean the gravelly bottom. Several thousand eggs are then emitted in the shallow depression created, and fertilized by the male. The male stand guard attempting to fend off intruders. It is less prolific than say, bluegills, and therefore poses less of an over-population problem.

Angling Tips

Use live bait rather than artificial lures. The hopeful angler can try a wet or dry fly, but if you're out to catch lunch in a hurry, use earthworms, shrimp, nightcrawlers, or grasshoppers. Spincasting will bring good results if you fish near the surface, and the cane pole will always work.

REDEAR SUNFISH

State	Frequency	Average Size lbs.-ozs.	Record lbs.-ozs.	Year
Alabama	abundant	0 – 6	4 – 4	1962
Florida	abundant	—	—	—
Illinois	present	—	2 – 0	1971
Indiana	present	—	2 – 11	1964
Kentucky	present	—	2 – 5	1964
Louisiana	present	0 – 8	—	—
Missouri	present	0 – 8	1 – 3	1971
Nebraska	present	—	1 – 6	1970
North Carolina	present	—	—	—
South Dakota	present	—	—	—
Texas	present	—	1 – 12½	1969
Virginia	abundant	—	4 – 8	1970

GOLDEYE

Other names: Winnipeg goldeye.

This famous freshwater panfish is better known for its commercial purposes than as a sport fish, but it is excellent for fly fishermen.

Appearance

The goldeye has largish silvery, shiny scales with large gold or yellow-colored eyes.

Spawning Habits

There is still some mystery about how the goldeye spawns, because occasionally the female will carry her eggs into the next season. Others drop them over rocky or gravelly beds in fairly shallow water.

Angling Tips

In Canada there is a substantial comercial market for Winnipeg goldeye, which ironically is taken mostly in the province of Alberta. It is smoked, and has been a national dish for over 100 years.

Anglers wishing to try their luck should use wet or dry flies, a baited hook or a small spinner. They prefer shallow, turbid waters, and will vigorously hit almost anything presented. Unhappily the population is declining as the demand for the smoked variety grows. Unsmoked, the goldeye is not pleasant eating.

GOLDEYE

State or Province	Frequency	Average Size lbs.-ozs.	Record lbs.-ozs.	Year
Arkansas	present	0 – 8	—	—
Illinois	present	0 – 8	—	—
Indiana	present	—	—	—
Iowa	abundant	—	—	—
Kansas	present	0 – 4	1 – 8	1970
Louisiana	present	0 – 6	—	—
Minnesota	present	—	—	—
Montana	abundant	—	—	—
North Dakota	abundant	2 – 0	—	—
Ohio	present	0 – 8	—	—
Oklahoma	present	0 – 8	—	—
South Dakota	abundant	—	2 – 2½	—
Tennessee	present	0 – 8	—	—
West Virginia	present	0 – 4	2 – 12	1963
Wyoming	present	2 – 0	—	—
CANADA				
Alberta	present	0 – 8	4 – 0	1967
British Columbia	present	0 – 8	—	—
Manitoba	present	—	3 – 0	1970
N.W. Territories	present	—	—	—
Saskatchewan	present	—	—	—

LAKE WHITEFISH

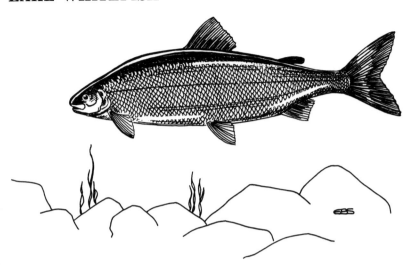

Other names: Great Lakes whitefish.

Essentially a deep water fish, the lake whitefish is difficult to catch during the summer, requiring much patience, long lines, and luck. In the winter the results can be far more productive for ice fishermen.

It is not an exciting fish to catch and requires some planning for effective execution. The exception is in northern rivers where it rises to a dry fly and fights extremely well. The whitefish does not hit the bait, but sort of sucks it in, making it difficult for the fisherman to know when he has a strike. Setting the hook needs only a delicate pull, for the mouth of the whitefish is tender and can be torn easily.

During the season ice fishermen regularly "chum" their holes with shiners, kept alive in a cage, or with salted minnows. Tidbits such as chopped burbot flesh, cooked rice, or other grains, are also scattered on the bottom.

The whitefish is deep and compressed. It has a silvery sheen with an olive brown back. The head is small, short and blunted; the back arched. The scales are large and smooth. Spawning is achieved in shallow water, but this is about the only time it comes close to the surface.

Its main value apart from the contribution it makes to ice fishermen is commercial, being an extremely valuable commodity. The roe from whitefish is made into caviar.

LAKE WHITEFISH

State or Province	Frequency	Average Size lbs.-ozs.	Record lbs.-ozs.	Year
Colorado	present	2 – 0	—	—
Indiana	present	—	—	—
Maine	abundant	2 – 8	7 – 8	1958
Michigan	present	4 – 0	25 – 3	1946
Minnesota	abundant	—	—	—
Montana	present	—	—	—
New Hampshire	present	1 – 8	—	—
New York	present	—	—	—
Ohio	present	—	—	—
Pennsylvania	present	—	—	—
Washington	present	—	—	—
Wisconsin	abundant	4 – 0	—	—
CANADA				
Alberta	present	1 – 0	6 – 11	1966
British Columbia	present	2 – 0	—	—
Manitoba	abundant	—	8 – 4	1959
New Brunswick	present	2 – 0	—	—
Newfoundland	abundant	1 – 8	—	—
Northwest Territories	abundant			
Ontario	abundant	1 – 8	—	—
Quebec	present	2 – 0	—	—
Saskatchewan	abundant	2 – 0	6 – 0	1971
Yukon	abundant	—	—	—

CATFISH

There are some 50 North American species of the catfish, with such diverse names as channel catfish, brown, yellow and black bullheads, lake catfish, cat, squealer, fiddler, forktail, flat head, speckled catfish, and silver catfish.

The catfish, so named for its whiskered chin, is widely appreciated in North America, particularly the southern United States, as a sport fish offering excellent eating qualities.

CHANNEL CATFISH

Spawning Habits

The channel catfish spawns in the spring seeking out shallow waters in lakes or streams. The male guards the site until the eggs hatch and then watches over the young ones till they can fend for themselves.

Appearance

The chanel cat sports a small head, large eyes, and a deeply forked caudal or tail fin. Some eight whiskers, called barbels, are present under the chin and at the corners of the mouth. The skin is without apparent scale and the dorsal and pectoral fins carry sharp, painful spines. The body is dark and the sides greenish-grey.

Angling Tips

The channel catfish, as with the others of the same species, can withstand a much wider variety of water conditions than the elite trout/salmon families. Other members of the catfish family tend to inhabit slow, even sluggish and frequently muddy waters, but his cousin prefers slightly swifter and colder waters which occur more frequently in Canada. The barbels or whiskers give the catfish a superior sensory system which they use on the bottom to seek out food. Ironically, the catfish aren't terribly selective about what they eat. And sometimes old cigaret butts will fill the bill.

Channel cats feed heavily at night and therefore the wise angler will place his bait out at this time. A strong rod, plenty of line and sinkers, and bait will sufice. Drop the bait almost to the bottom and let the exotic barbels smell the food. Then be prepared for a good tug-of-war with these extraordinary creatures. The fight will be virgorous but not spectacular, unless you have a 60 pounder on the line.

The varied range of bait includes worms, bait fish, chunks of meat, chewing gum, soap, and chunks of fish. Despite its incredible diet, the flesh is sweet and clean, thanks probably to a superior digestive system which processes out the pollutant materials.

Channel cats can be taken on lures and spinning tackle but bait fishing is by far the most popular and most successful method. Stillfishing at night with a wide assortment of bait will bring good results.

CHANNEL CATFISH

State or Province	Frequency	Average Size lbs.-ozs.	Record lbs.-ozs.	Year
Alabama	abundant	1 – 0	—	—
Arizona	abundant	—	35 – 4	1952
Arkansas	abundant	2 – 8	13 – 0	1963
California	present	5 – 0	40 – 8	1971
Colorado	abundant	4 – 0	25 – 9	1962
Connecticut	present	1 – 8	—	—
Delaware	present	2 – 0	—	—
Florida	abundant	—	—	—
Georgia	abundant	2 – 0	39 – 3	1969
Idaho	present	—	21 – 8	1970
Illinois	present	1 – 0	28 – 0	1963
Indiana	abundant	—	27 – 0	1970
Iowa	abundant	—	25 – 3	1964
Kansas	abundant	2 – 0	32 – 0	1962
Kentucky	abundant	1 – 8	—	—
Louisiana	abundant	2 – 8	62 – 0	1970
Maryland	abundant	1 – 8	18 – 0	1960
Massachusetts	present	—	13 – 8	1964
Michigan	abundant	3 – 0	47 – 8	1937
Minnesota	present	2 – 0	37 – 0	—
Mississippi	abundant	3 – 8	—	—
Missouri	abundant	2 – 0	29 – 12	1969
Montana	present	—	—	—
Nebraska	abundant	—	31 – 12	1944
Nevada	present	0 – 8	21 – 8	1968
New Jersey	present	—	28 – 0	1918
New Mexico	present	2 – 8	17 – 12	1971
New York	present	—	—	—
North Carolina	abundant	1 – 8	23 – 4	1970
North Dakota	abundant	1 – 12	26 – 8	1968
Ohio	abundant	2 – 0	25 – 0	1964
Oklahoma	abundant	1 – 0	20 – 2	1968
Oregon	present	4 – 0	29 – 0	—
Pennsylvania	abundant	—	35 – 0	1970
South Carolina	abundant	—	58 – 0	1964
South Dakota	abundant	—	55 – 0	1949
Tennessee	abundant	0 – 12	24 – 2	1967
Texas	abundant	3 – 0	36 – 8	1965
Utah	present	—	—	—
Vermont	present	4 – 0	21 – 4	1969

CHANNEL CATFISH (Continued)

State or Province	Frequency	Average Size lbs.-ozs.	Record lbs.-ozs.	Year
Virginia	abundant	—	26 – 0	1966
Washington	present	—	8 – 14	1970
West Virginia	abundant	2 – 0	19 – 0	1963
Wisconsin	abundant	2 – 0	44 – 0	1962
Wyoming	present	2 – 0	18 – 0	1946
CANADA				
Manitoba	present	—	—	—
Ontario	abundant	10 – 0	37 – 0	—

BLUE CATFISH

Other names: Chucklehead, forktail, Mississippi blue catfish.

This largest of the catfish clan is avidly sought in southern climes, but is found as far north as Ontario.

The average weight ranges from one to 10 pounds, but several catches of 100 pounds have been recorded.

Appearance

Look for the tell-tale barbels or whiskers on the jaws, the deeply forked tail, and the murkly blue to grey top, shading off to a silvery white belly. Its anal fin contains some 36 rays and looks like an under-sided brush cut.

Spawning Habits

The male and female seek out secluded spots in sheltered areas, and after fertilization, stay on jointly to help bring up the young.

Angling Tips

The big blue prefers clean, fast-flowing streams and is found frequently on the bottom. A large variety of natural bait can be used, ranging from a string of nightcrawlers on an 8/0 salt water hook, to clams, various kinds of meat, or the guts of animals, dead birds, frogs, mice or chicks. Artificial lures can be used but the most successful catfish angler will choose natural bait.

Angling is best between mid-spring and late fall. Late evening is most productive, when the cat leaves its lair to seek out food. Fishing during the daylight hours compels you to stalk this master in deep pools, underhangs, and beneath rocks. If you're unlucky the first few times around, change the natural bait; there's no telling what the cat had last for dinner and what it wants now.

If it's hooked on the bottom, be prepared for a long drawn-out fight as the blue catfish tries to disgorge the offending hook. Nearer

136

the surface, it can cause quite a splash as it attempts to get away. Drop lines, hand lines and trot lines are legal in some states, as is "grabbling", which means grabbing the catfish with bare hands.

Whatever way you take it, the blue catfish makes good eating. Remember the cat must be skinned, and this can be done by cutting around the head, down the back, and then using pliers to pull the skin off.

BLUE CATFISH

State or Province	Frequency	Average Size lbs.-ozs.	Record lbs.-ozs.	Year
Alabama	abundant	3 – 0	58 – 0	1971
Arizona	present	—	—	—
Arkansas	abundant	5 – 0	47 – 8	1970
California	present	0 – 8	—	—
Colorado	present	8 – 0	—	—
Illinois	present	2 – 0	65 – 0	1956
Indiana	abundant	—	50 – 0	1970
Iowa	present	—	—	—
Kansas	present	—	—	—
Kentucky	abundant	5 – 0	100 – 0	1970
Louisiana	abundant	3 – 8	—	—
Maryland	present	3 – 0	24 – 0	1964
Mississippi	present	10 – 0	—	—
Missouri	present	5 – 0	56 – 0	1961
Nebraska	present	—	100 – 8	1970
New Mexico	present	—	—	—
North Carolina	present	—	—	—
Ohio	present	0 – 8	—	—
Oklahoma	present	5 – 0	37 – 0	1969
South Carolina	present	—	—	—
South Dakota	present	—	100 – 8	—
Tennessee	abundant	0 – 12	—	—
Texas	abundant	10 – 0	—	—
Washington	present	—	14 – 10	1970
West Virginia	present	3 – 0	—	—
CANADA				
Ontario	present	4 – 0	—	—

FLATHEAD CATFISH

Other names: Yellow cat, mud cat.

The flathead trails only a few pounds behind the blue catfish in size, the biggest state record being 86 pounds, three ounces in Kanasas.

Appearance

The flathead catfish has a greenish-brown back with brown spots or blotches on the sides. It has the characteristic barbels described in earlier chapters. It differs dramatically from the blue catfish in the tail, which is flat, compared to the deep fork in the blue. Its lower jaw is always longer than the upper and there are white marks on the caudal fin.

Angling Tips

You'll find this tasty creature lying quietly in deep, sluggish pools in the larger rivers, and occasionally it makes its way to shallower waters if feeding is poor.

Hand lines and trot lines are successful with this one, although the other devices spelled out in the previous chapter are also useful with the flathead. Remember to have a variety of natural bait around to test the fish's wants that particular day. Once hooked it heads to deeper water, so make sure the bait is fully mouthed before attempting to set the hook.

FLATHEAD CATFISH

State	Frequency	Average Size lbs.-ozs.	Record lbs.-ozs.	Year
Arizona	present	—	65 – 0	1951
Idaho	present	—	—	—
Illinois	present	—	51 – 0	1950
Kansas	present	—	86 – 3	1966
Kentucky	present	—	97 – 0	1956
Minnesota	present	—	70 – 0	—
Missouri	present	—	61 – 0	1963
Nebraska	present	—	59 – 0	1961
New Mexico	present	15 – 0	62 – 0	1970
South Dakota	present	—	36 – 0	—
Texas	present	—	—	—
Virginia	present	—	45 – 0	1967
Wisconsin	present	20 – 0	61 – 0	1966

BROWN AND BLACK BULLHEAD

Other names: Bullpout, horned pout.

These are the most common of the catfish family, although much smaller than the channel cats. The average weight varies from 4-ounces to 3-pounds, with widespread distribution throughout the continent.

Spawning Habits

The bullhead spawns in warm, sluggish waters, after scraping out a depression in the mud. As with their channel cousins, these fish guard the fry until they can safely make their own way in the murky habitat.

Appearance

Uglier than the channel cat, they sport whiskers or barbels protruding from mouth and chin. The tail fin is square and sharp, and spines are present in the dorsal and pectoral fins.

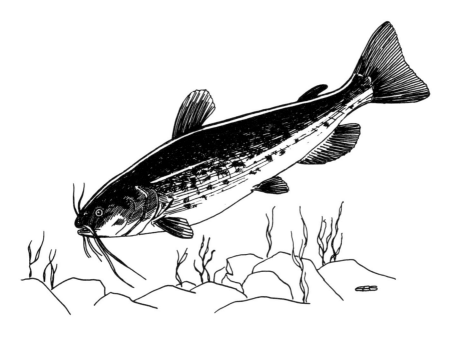

The brown bullhead is yellow-brown to chocolate-brown on the back, sliding off to yellow or milky white on the belly. There may be a splotchy appearance to the scaleless skin.

The black bullhead's barbels are dark, and there are no serrations on their pectoral spines. The back can range from black to green, its flanks are yellow to white, and the belly is creamy colored.

BROWN BULLHEAD

State or Province	Frequency	Average Size lbs.-ozs.	Record lbs.-ozs.	Year
Alabama	abundant	0 – 6	—	—
Arizona	present	—	—	—
Arkansas	abundant	0 – 8	—	—
California	present	0 – 8	—	—
Colorado	present	0 – 8	—	—
Connecticut	abundant	0 – 8	2 – 14	1968
Georgia	abundant	1 – 0	—	—
Idaho	present	0 – 8	—	—

139

BROWN BULLHEAD (Continued)

State or Province	Frequency	Average Size lbs.-ozs.	Record lbs.-ozs.	Year
Illinois	present	0 – 8	—	—
Indiana	abundant	—	—	—
Iowa	abundant	—	—	—
Kansas	present	0 – 4	—	—
Kentucky	abundant	0 – 8	—	—
Louisiana	abundant	1 – 0	—	—
Maine	abundant	0 – 8	—	—
Massachusetts	abundant	—	5 – 8	1965
Michigan	present	—	—	—
Minnesota	abundant	—	—	—
Mississippi	present	0 – 8	—	—
Missouri	abundant	0 – 10	—	—
Nebraska	present	—	—	—
Nevada	present	—	—	—
New Hampshire	abundant	0 – 6	—	—
New Jersey	abundant	—	22 – 15	1966
New Mexico	present	0 – 6	—	—
New York	abundant	—	—	—
North Carolina	present	—	—	—
Ohio	abundant	0 – 5	3 – 14¾	1966
Oklahoma	present	0 – 4	—	—
Oregon	abundant	1 – 0	—	—
Pennsylvania	abundant	—	11 – 8	1966
Rhode Island	abundant	0 – 8	—	—
South Carolina	abundant	3 – 0	5 – 0	1970
South Dakota	present	—	—	—
Tennessee	present	0 – 5	—	—
Vermont	abundant	0 – 8	1 – 8	1969
Virginia	abundant	—	—	—
Washington	present	0 – 10	—	—
West Virginia	abundant	0 – 4	—	—
Wisconsin	abundant	1 – 0	2 – 3	1971
CANADA				
Alberta	present	0 – 8	—	—
British Columbia	present	0 – 8	—	—
Manitoba	present	—	—	—
New Brunswick	abundant	0 – 6	—	—
Newfoundland	present	0 – 8	—	—
Nova Scotia	abundant	0 – 8	—	—
Ontario	present	0 – 8	—	—

BLACK BULLHEAD

State or Province	Frequency	Average Size lbs.-ozs.	Record lbs.-ozs.	Year
Alabama	abundant	—	—	—
Arizona	present	—	—	—
Arkansas	abundant	0 – 8	—	—
California	present	—	—	—

140

State or Province	Frequency	Average Size lbs.-ozs.	Record lbs.-ozs.	Year
Colorado	abundant	0 – 4	—	—
Georgia	present	—	—	—
Idaho	present	—	—	—
Illinois	present	0 – 4	3 – 7	1970
Indiana	abundant	—	3 – 9	1966
Iowa	abundant	—	—	—
Kansas	abundant	0 – 4	4 – 3½	1961
Kentucky	abundant	0 – 8	—	—
Louisiana	abundant	1 – 0	—	—
Massachusetts	present	—	5 – 9	1963
Michigan	abundant	—	—	—
Minnesota	abundant	—	—	—
Mississippi	abundant	0 – 8	2 – 10	1970
Missouri	abundant	0 – 8	2 – 14½	1971
Montana	present	—	—	—
Nebraska	abundant	—	3 – 8	1963
Nevada	present	—	—	—
New Hampshire	present	0 – 6	—	—
New Mexico	abundant	0 – 4	—	—
New York	present	—	8 – 0	1951
North Dakota	abundant	0 – 4	—	—
Ohio	abundant	0 – 4	—	—
Oklahoma	present	0 – 4	—	—
Oregon	abundant	1 – 0	—	—
Pennsylvania	present	—	—	—
South Dakota	abundant	—	3 – 0	—
Tennessee	present	0 – 5	—	—
Texas	abundant	0 – 4	—	—
Utah	abundant	—	—	—
Vermont	present	—	—	—
Virginia	abundant	—	—	—
West Virginia	abundant	0 – 4	3 – 0	1964
Wisconsin	abundant	0 – 4	2 – 9	1967
Wyoming	present	0 – 4	—	—
CANADA				
Alberta	present	—	—	—
British Columbia	present	0 – 8	—	—
Manitoba	present	—	—	—
Ontario	abundant	0 – 8	—	—
Quebec	present	—	—	—

ROCK BASS

Other names: Red eye, northern rock bass, black perch, rock sunfish and goggle-eye.

This easy-to-land member of the sunfish family, as the name so aptly suggests, lurks in many fresh-flowing rocky streams or the rocky shallows of lakes.

Appearance

The rock bass has a deep, flattened, somewhat oblong body, showing shades of olive green on the sides. The sides are mottled with brownish or coppery-colored spots or blotches. On the end of each scale is a little black spot which taken together may give the appearance of a series of stripes along the body. The eye is red and the mouth extends beyond it. The two-part dorsal fin is composed of some 11 or 12 sharp rays in the front, followed by a grouping of soft rays. The anal fin has six spines, which makes a useful distinguishing feature.

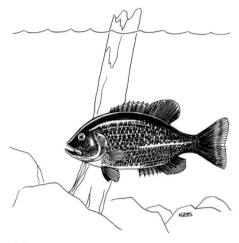

Spawning Habits

Like other sunfish, the rock bass nests in shallow, gravelly or sandy bottoms, and spawning starts when the temperature reaches between 60 to 70 degrees. The male guards the nest with the usual sunfish attention to the young, and when not guarding moves in schools with his brethren.

Angling Tips

The rock bass rarely refuses bait any time of the day or night, so you can choose your weapon from a wide range. Everything from a popping bug to minnows, crayfish, crickets, grasshoppers, all kinds of worms, and even hellgrammites. They tend to be found in smallmouth territory, so casting your line in rocky areas of streams and lakes should bring good results. Wet or dry flies, and bass bugs are also effective, although the flies must be allowed to sink with each cast. The rock bass puts up a short, swift fight, then tires and can be landed quickly and safely.

Candidly, landing a rock bass is often the byproduct of fishing for something else, usually a bronze back. Few experienced anglers seek them out purposefully, but take them as they come. This fish starts to bite early in the spring and carries on well into the fall. In fact he often substitutes for smallmouth or trout when the latter two refuse to bite. Rock bass are good to eat either in the spring or late fall from cold, clear water, but the taste deteriorates if you take them from warm muddy habitat.

ROCK BASS

State or Province	Frequency	Average Size lbs.-ozs.	Record lbs.-ozs.	Year
Alabama	abundant	0 – 5	—	—
Arizona	present	—	—	—
Arkansas	abundant	0 – 6	1 – 6½	1963
Colorado	present	0 – 4	—	—
Connecticut	abundant	0 – 6	—	—
Georgia	present	—	—	—
Illinois	present	0 – 5	1 – 9	1968
Indiana	abundant	—	3 – 0	1969
Iowa	abundant	—	—	—
Kentucky	abundant	—	—	—
Louisiana	abundant	0 – 12	—	—
Maryland	abundant	0 – 4	0 – 13	1951
Massachusetts	present	—	—	—
Michigan	abundant	0 – 8	3 – 10	1965
Minnesota	abundant	—	—	—
Mississippi	present	0 – 5	—	—
Missouri	present	0 – 6	2 – 12	1968
Montana	present	—	—	—
Nebraska	present	—	2 – 0	1966
New Hampshire	present	0 – 4	—	—
New Jersey	present	—	1 – 4	1932
New Mexico	present	—	—	—
New York	abundant	—	—	—
North Carolina	present	0 – 6	—	—
North Dakota	present	—	—	—
Ohio	abundant	0 – 5	1 – 15½	1962
Oklahoma	present	0 – 4	—	—
Pennsylvania	abundant	—	3 – 0	1966
South Carolina	abundant	—	—	—
South Dakota	present	—	1 – 3	—
Tennessee	abundant	0 – 5	2 – 8	1958
Texas	present	0 – 12	—	—
Vermont	abundant	—	—	—
Virginia	abundant	—	2 – 2	1964
West Virginia	abundant	0 – 4	1 – 11	1964
Wisconsin	abundant	0 – 4	1 – 12	1971
Wyoming	present	—	—	—

State or Province CANADA	Frequency	Average Size lbs.-ozs.	Record lbs.-ozs.	Year
Alberta	present	0 – 8	—	—
British Columbia	present	1 – 0	—	—
Manitoba	present	—	—	—
Newfoundland	present	0 – 8	—	—
Ontario	present	0 – 8	—	—
Quebec	present	—	—	—
Saskatchewan	abundant	—	—	—

SPOTTED BASS

Other names: Kentucky spotted bass.

This fish falls fairly neatly between the largemouth and small-mouth bass in nearly every classification, and in fact was only identified as a distinct member of the clan 40-odd years ago.

Appearance

Its name suggests its appearance, and along the lateral line one sees diamond-shaped spots; below this line are rows of dark splotches, and on the back less-distinct diamond-shaped spots. The basic topside color is olive green and the partially forked caudal fin sports white, black, and orangey-red markings. It differs from its largemouth and smallmouth cousins in that the lower jaw doesn't extend past the eye, nor does it have bars vertically along its flanks as with the latter.

Spawning Habits

The spotted bass breeds upstream as it migrates toward head-waters. It chooses shallower waters, not more than 20 feet, to make nests much like the bigmouth and bronze backs. The male drives various females into the nest and after spawning sends them away. The spotted bass does not usually administer any care to the eggs, leaving them to the elements.

Angling Tips

Fish for a spotted bass much as you would for a smallmouth, in early spring and early fall. It feeds heavily morning and evening, but will hit a lure pretty well around the clock. The spotted bass prefers more sluggish waters. It is predominant in the south where it can also be found in smallmouth territory. It will put up a vigorous fight and hit a variety of natural or artificial lures. You will probably have to shop around with everything from surface plugs to deep-running spoons.

SPOTTED BASS

State	Frequency	Average Size lbs.-ozs.	Record lbs.-ozs.	Year
Alabama	abundant	0 – 12	8 – 8	1968
Arkansas	abundant	0 – 12	6 – 9	1971
California	present	1 – 8	—	—
Georgia	abundant	2 – 0	7 – 8	1969
Illinois	present	1 – 0	1 – 13	1971
Indiana	abundant	—	4 – 9	1970
Kansas	abundant	0 – 8	3 – 15¼	1970
Kentucky	abundant	1 – 0	7 – 10	1970
Louisiana	abundant	—	4 – 3	—
Mississippi	abundant	1 – 8	7 – 14	1965
Missouri	present	1 – 0	7 – 8	1966
Nebraska	present	—	3 – 11	1968
North Carolina	present	1 – 0	—	—
Ohio	present	1 – 8	5 – 4	1967
Oklahoma	present	1 – 0	8 – 2	1958
Tennessee	abundant	0 – 10	5 – 2	1971
Texas	abundant	2 – 0	4 – 8	1968
Virginia	present	—	2 – 4	1970
West Virginia	present	0 – 12	3 – 2	1966

STRIPED BASS

Other names: Striper, greenhead.

This coastal fish is avidly sought by expert and amateur anglers, and has successfully been transplanted inland. In fact, as the accompanying chart shows, the striper appears in many parts of the continent. One of the attractions is its love for the gizzard shad, which helps keep that population within reason. To avoid confusion in the chart, the average size and record columns indicate whether the catch was taken in coastal waters or inland.

Appearance

There are no problems in recognizing this creature. There are 7 to 8 distinct horizontal, dark stripes along the sides with two distinct, unconnected, triangular, even dorsal fins, the first group spiny, the second group soft. The back is olive green to blue, shading to silver on the flanks and white below. The striper has a long head and a strong but not pointed snout.

Spawning Habits

The sea-going female striper is ready for spawning anywhere from her fourth to sixth year while the male is ready in two to three. Starting in late spring in the south (and up to July in the northern waters), the striper enters the rivers from its saltwater habitat and

145

can go as much as 100 miles inland. The female picks a spot where the flow of water is quick, clean and cold, then is surrounded by males. During the ensuing horseplay, the female emits anywhere from 50,000 to 5,000,000 eggs, depending on age. The eggs flow free and are on their own in the current. Hatching occurs when the temperature is right.

Angling Tips

For sea-run stripers, surf-casting, trolling and plug-casting are effective, with heavy artificial lures or clams, crabs, eels, or even squid if you can get it. Landlocked striped bass are normally boated by deep trolling with plugs and spinners.

Gizzard shad, as mentioned, is an attractive bait and can be used when still-fishing. As the weights on the charts indicate, make sure your line is strong enough before going after the lunkers. With anywhere up to 44-pound stripers in veiw, use 20-40 pound test with heavy spinning or bait-casting rods. If you have patience and a sense of adventure combined, try to catch one when it feeds at the top, during the spring or late summer. When the striper goes after shad, the angler has to work fast with either a popper or spoon because the surface activity may only last for minutes.

STRIPED BASS [Sea-going and (S) and landlocked (L)]

State or Province	Frequency	Average Size lbs.-ozs.	Record lbs.-ozs.	Year
Arizona (L)	present	—	38 – 12	1969
Arkansas (L)	abundant	3 – 0	40 – 0	1971
California (S)	abundant	—	—	—
Connecticut (S)	present	—	—	—
Florida (S)	present	—	—	—
Kansas (L)	present	—	9 – 9	1971
Kentucky (L)	abundant	7 – 0	44 – 4	1970
Louisiana (L)	abundant	2 – 8	—	—
Massachusetts (S)	abundant	—	73 – 0	1913
Missouri (L)	present	—	5 – 12	1970
Mississippi (L)	abundant	—	—	—
Nebraska (L)	present	—	10 – 1	1970
Nevada (L)	present	10 – 0	24 – 0	1969
New Jersey (S)	abundant	—	—	—
New York (S)	abundant	—	—	—
North Carolina (S)	abundant	—	125 – 0	*1891
Oklahoma (L)	present	1 – 0	20 – 2	1971
Oregon (S)	present	—	—	—
South Carolina (S) & (L)	abundant	15 – 0	55 – 0	1963
Tennessee (L)	abundant	—	—	—
Texas (L)	present	—	12 – 12	1969

State or Province	Frequency	Average Size lbs.-ozs.	Record lbs.-ozs.	Year
Virginia (S) .... present		—	32 – 3	—
Washington (S) .... present		—	—	—
CANADA				
New Brunswick (S) .... present		—	—	—
Nova Scotia (S) .... present		5 – 0	20 – 0+	—
Prince Edward Is. (S) .. present		—	30 – 0+	—
Quebec (S) .... present		6 – 0	16 – 11	1963

*This 80-year old record has never been approached and a 75-pound sea-run striper would make a contemporary record.

WHITE BASS

Other names: Silver bass.

This true member of the bass family has increased in importance as a sport fish. (The other fresh water member is the yellow bass). This rise in popularity is due in part to its fine flesh and also its eagerness to take the lure.

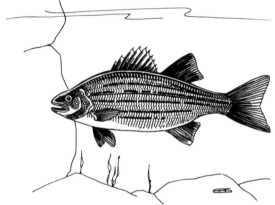

Appearance

The first spiny fin is clearly separated from the second row of soft rays. The back is dark grey in color changing to silver on the sides and yellow to white on the belly. There are 5 to 7 lateral stripes which can lend momentary confusion with the striped bass, and the eye can have a yellow tint to it. In typical bass fashion, the lower jaw projects beyond the upper jaw.

Spawning Habits

The white bass spawns in the spring, in shallow water near the shore or on gravelly shoals. The eggs are left to fend alone and can hatch in 2 to 5 days depending on the temperature, which is critical to its survival. In fact the survival rate is so low that the fish fluctu-

ates in abundance from year to year, depending on the success of
the spawning.

Angling Tips

The white bass prefers large lakes, and larger rivers. During most
of the day it spends its time in deep water, but towards evening may
swim to the shore in tightly controlled schools to vigorously attack
any small fish in the neighborhood. It is here that the alert angler
will deploy his spiners, small plugs, flies or spoons for splashy action.
Cast into the midst of the feeding school and watch the water fly.

WHITE BASS

State or Province	Frequency	Average Size lbs.-ozs.	Record lbs.-ozs.	Year
Alabama	abundant	0 – 8	4 – 2	1971
Arizona	present	—	4 – 10½	1966
Arkansas	abundant	0 – 12	4 – 15	1969
California	present	0 – 10	3 – 11	1971
Colorado	present	1 – 0	2 – 14	1969
Georgia	abundant	1 – 8	5 – 1	1971
Illinois	present	0 – 8	4 – 1	1970
Indiana	present	—	4 – 3	1965
Iowa	abundant	—	3 – 7	1970
Kansas	present	0 – 6	5 – 4	1966
Kentucky	abundant	1 – 8	5 – 0	1943 and 1957
Louisiana	present	—	3 – 14	1969
Mississippi	present	1 – 0	5 – 2	1960
Missouri	abundant	1 – 0	4 – 8	1952
Nebraska	abundant	—	4 – 15	1962
Nevada	present	1 – 0	3 – 1	1969
New Mexico	abundant	0 – 10	3 – 4	1971
New York	abundant	—	—	—
North Carolina	abundant	0 – 8	—	—
North Dakota	abundant	1 – 8	3 – 4	1969
Ohio	abundant	0 – 12	3 – 6	1954
Oklahoma	abundant	0 – 10	4 – 14	1969
Pennsylvania	present	—	—	—
South Carolina	abundant	2 – 0	—	—
South Dakota	abundant	—	4 – 0	—
Tennessee	abundant	0 – 12	4 – 10	1949
Texas	abundant	1 – 8	5 – 4¼	1968
Utah	present	0 – 8	—	—
Virginia	present	—	3 – 6	1971
West Virginia	present	1 – 0	4 – 0	1964
Wisconsin	abundant	1 – 0	3 – 9	1962
CANADA				
Manitoba	present	—	—	—
Ontario	abundant	1 – 0	—	—

CARP

Other names: German carp, European carp, mirror carp, leather carp, golden carp, mudhog and bugle-mouthed bass.

The carp, an enormously popular European fish, was imported to North America as early as 1832, and by the turn of the century had spread virtually across the continent.

It has a mixed reputation with sport fishermen; some say its spawning habits disturb the placid waters, and its quality as a table fish is questioned by others. But carefully prepared, it can make a tasty dinner. Its fighting spirit is hardy but doesn't make for the spectacular kinds of thrills offered by other game fish. Nonetheless the carp is becoming more and more popular, equalling the esteem with which it is held in Europe.

Appearance

The two barbels or whiskers which protrude from each side of the jaw are the single most distinguishing feature of tis fish. It has one strong spiny ray in its dorsal fin followed by 16 to 20 soft rays. The scales are so marked as to give the sides the appearance of being seen through a vivid latice-work or cross-hatch. The coloration is olive green turning to yellow on the belly.

Spawning Habits

The carp spawns in the late spring with much rooting about in the vegetation. The fish selects shallow, weedy areas of protected bays or backwaters and proceeds to thrash about, causing great commotion and uprooting adjacent underwater vegetation. The eggs are emitted with an adhesive coating which are then fertilized by the male and deserted by both parents.

Angling Tips

For a fish that can go as high as 74 pounds, stout tackle is required. A one or two-handed fresh water spinning reel or bait-casting rod is suitable to landing this beast. While it will take artificial lures, most carp fishermen are successful with natural bait, including the famous — or infamous as some would have it — doughballs. These are composed of a mash made by adding equal parts of corn meal to boiling water, stirring, adding sugar, and cooling. The resulting sticky mess is then kneeded and stored or used as the occasion demands. A trip to the local pizza house can save time. To bait the hook, put the dough on the tip of the hook.

Use No. 1 or 2 hooks for small fish, No. 2/0 to 5/0 for larger fish. You may put the dough just on the tip of the hook or right up to the eye, forming a pear-shaped attraction. Other popular baits include bread, corn, peas, potatoes, various kinds of meat, clams, crayfish, worms or whatever is left-over from dinner.

After a winter's respite from feeding, the carp is eager for action in the spring. Look for lakes or ponds with muddy bottoms or sluggish streams and backwaters, then present the bait as quietly as possible. Make sure the creature has enough time to mouth the bait before attempting to set the hook. After setting the hook let the powerful fish run until it's exhausted. While the fight lacks the grace of a hooked rainbow, it is vigorous and can keep an angler on his toes until its finally boated.

Carp are also fished with bow and arrow or with spears, depending on local state regulations. Make sure you check your favorite fish cooking book for the right recipe before putting it on the plate.

CARP

State or Province	Frequency	Average Size lbs.-ozs.	Record lbs.-ozs.	Year
Alabama	abundant	3 – 0	16 – 11	1964
Arizona	abundant	—	—	—
Arkansas	abundant	5 – 0	—	—
California	abundant	4 – 0	52 – 0	1968
Colorado	present	2 – 0	—	—
Connecticut	abundant	8 – 0	—	—
Delaware	abundant	3 – 0	—	—
Florida	present	—	—	—
Georgia	abundant	2 – 0	35 – 6	1967
Idaho	present	—	—	—
Illinois	present	3 – 0	42 – 0	1928
Indiana	abundant	—	38 – 1	1967
Iowa	abundant	—	50 – 0	1969
Kansas	abundant	3 – 0	35 – 4	1970
Kentucky	abundant	3 – 0	54 – 14	1971
Louisiana	abundant	5 – 0	—	—
Maine	present	6 – 0	—	—
Maryland	abundant	3 – 8	44 – 0	1970
Massachusetts	present	—	—	—
Michigan	abundant	4 – 0	38 – 4	1971
Minnesota	abundant	—	55 – 5	1952
Mississippi	abundant	3 – 0	74 – 0	1963
Missouri	abundant	2 – 8	41 – 0	1969
Montana	abundant	—	—	—
Nebraska	abundant	—	28 – 2	1967
Nevada	present	—	—	—

State or Province	Frequency	Average Size lbs.-ozs.	Record lbs.-ozs.	Year
New Hampshire	present	5 – 8	21 – 0	1969
New Jersey	abundant	—	—	—
New Mexico	abundant	—	—	—
New York	abundant	—	—	—
North Carolina	abundant	4 – 0	—	—
North Dakota	abundant	3 – 0	21 – 12	1958
Ohio	abundant	3 – 0	50 – 0	1967
Oklahoma	present	2 – 0	32 – 12	1968
Oregon	present	—	—	—
Pennsylvania	abundant	—	52 – 0	1962
Rhode Island	abundant	3 – 0	—	—
South Carolina	abundant	—	—	—
South Dakota	abundant	—	—	—
Tennessee	abundant	3 – 0	—	—
Texas	abundant	4 – 0	23 – 12	1968
Utah	abundant	3 – 8	—	—
Vermont	present	—	—	—
Virginia	abundant	—	60 – 0	1970
West Virginia	abundant	4 – 0	40 – 0	1970
Wisconsin	abundant	5 – 0	57 – 2	1966
Wyoming	present	0 – 12	—	—

CANADA

Alberta	present	—	—	—
British Columbia	present	5 – 0	18 – 0	—
Manitoba	present	—	—	—
Ontario	abundant	4 – 0	—	—
Quebec	present	—	—	—

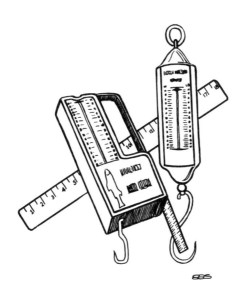

Chapter 20

The Great Fishing Holes

ALABAMA

Department of Conservation
Game and Fish Division
64 Union Street North
Montgomery, Alabama
Telephone for free information, call 1-800, 633-5761 to the Alabama Bureau of Publicity and information from anywhere in the U.S. excluding Alaska and Hawaii

Say Alabama and you say bass. The gentle seasons of spring and fall are the time to take them. Lake Eufaula offers renowned bass fishing and Lay Lake is another recommended spot. The level of this lake was raised a few years ago and the timber was left standing, so it supplies good crappie and bream fishing too. Millers Ferry Impoundment is a new site with an expanding population of bass and bream. Smith Lake not far from Birmingham has largemouth, some stocked rainbow trout and excellent spotted bass. An 8 lb. 8 oz. spotted bass was taken from this lake in 1968. There are 10 major rivers in Alabama. The Tennessee river has only smallmouth bass, but catfish are abundant. Bluegill are also plentiful in Alabama and Lake Ketona near Birmingham supplied a 4 lb. 12 oz. bluegill in 1950.

ALASKA

Sport Fish Division
Department of Fish & Game
Subport Building
Juneau 99081, Alaska

Alaska, land of the kodiak bear, the gold rush, northern lights and giant salmon seems romantic and faraway. Modern Alaska is, of course not so far away. The flying time from Seattle to Juneau is about three hours. One can take a more leisurely cruise up the coast

152

of British Columbia or drive through the wilderness of northern Canada, from Edmonton on the gravel-topped Alaska Highway.

Once there, the angler is in his own kind of paradise. There are in this State, in excess of 13,000 productive lakes with more than 7.3 million surface acres of water. There are some 366,000 miles of streams and rivers which cover more than 5,000,000 surface acres. The total estimated inland, productive, freshwater fish habitat is more than 12.4 million acres, which is nearly one half that of the rest of the United States, excluding the Great Lakes.

Fish sought are, the chinook salmon (king salmon) coho salmon, lake trout, cutthroat, dolly varden and rainbow trout. All are in abundance, as well as the Arctic grayling, Arctic char and the illusive sheefish or 'inconnu' (which means unknown.)

Much of the prime fishing water is still unsurveyed and inaccessible by road. The accepted mode of travel is the bush plane, and Alaska has more than 700 landing sites for aircraft.

ARIZONA

Arizona Game and Fish Department
2222 West Greenway Road
Phoenix 85023
Arizona

Late spring and early fall are the best times to fish for grayling, rainbow, native and brook trout from the lovely streams and lakes of the White Mountains of Eastern Arizona. There is fine trout fishing from these mountains right across the Mogollon Rim, with Canyon and Cibecue Creeks being noteworthy. Lake Powell in north central Arizona has rainbow trout, walleye and largemouth bass. Largemouth are in impoundments scattered through the desert country. San Carlos Lake and Roosevelt Lake are recommended. There are striped bass in the Colorado River and smallmouth bass are present in streams across the mid-section of the state.

ARKANSAS

State Game and Fish Commission
State Capital
Little Rock 72201
Arkansas

There is a war being waged between conservationists and the Corps of Engineers in Arkansas, with many dams having been constructed and more in the planning stage. There are 300 lakes and 9,000 miles of rivers and streams in the state with the following recommended: Upper White River, 100 miles of excellent rainbow habitat; Little Red River, 35 miles of trout waters; Arkansas River for largemouth bass and crappie; Greers Ferry for largemouths, white bass and walleye; Ouachita Lake in Ouachita National Forest for bigmouths and bronze backs as well as crappie; Bull Shoals for largemouth bass and Lake Greeson for stripers.

Millwood Lake is newly built in the southwest corner of the state offering crappie, bass, bluegill and bream fishing. DeGray has northern pike and largemouth bass, and Lake Conway is fished for bluegill, bream and bigmouth.

CALIFORNIA

Department of Fish and Game
721 Capitol Mall,
Sacramento, Calif. 95814

Most Californians think their state is paradise. Paradise must naturally, have an abundance of fish. California has. Freshwater game fish include seven varieties of trout; brown, cutthroat, rainbow, golden, brook, dolly varden and lakers. The salmon abundant in California waters are coho, or silver, kokanee, in some lakes and reservoirs, and chinook. The warm water fish that are present include large and smallmouth bass, walleye, yellow perch, bluegill, crappie and shad.

The Sacramento River near Castella, Shasta County, is one of the best rainbow streams in California but this fish is widely scattered over the state. Steelhead are found in most of the streams flowing into the Pacific from San Luis Obispo County north. The Smith River is the state's most northerly steelhead stream. Brown trout abound in Convict Lake, an inappropriate name for this beautiful lake nestled in mountains. Golden trout are present in California in a number of streams and lakes of the Sierra Nevada range from Alpine and El Dorado counties to the north to Inyo and Tulare counties to the south, generally at elevations over 8,000 feet. They are also in waters in Siskiyou and Trinity counties. These fish have been named the state fish.

Bighorn Lake in Fresno County is described as a typical golden trout habitat. The dolly varden is found in California only in the McCloud River below the lower falls and in the reservoirs connected with the river. The brook trout has become well established in alpine lakes and in the small streams of mountain meadows. It is most

154

commonly found at elevations between 5,000 and 9,000 feet. The lake trout is now present only in Lake Tahoe and Donner Lake. It does not enter the streams which flow into these waters. Kokanee have established self-perpetuating populations in 10 California lakes. Donner Lake is one of them.

Mountain whitefish is most common in the Truckee and Carson Rivers but may be found throughout the streams and lakes of the eastern slope of the Sierra Nevada. The Klamath River is recommended for Salmon fishing. The largemouth bass is abundant in California and is found throughout the state. Recommended are Clear Lake and Camanche Lake. Smallmouth bass may be caught in Putah Creek, the Russian River, lower portions of many tributaries of the Sacramento and San Joaquin Rivers and the Colorado River. Spotted bass can be found in a section of the Cosumnes River, Sacramento and El Dorado counties.

The bluegill is the most populous sunfish in California and is found in warm water lakes and in warm, slow moving streams. Redear have been stocked in farm ponds throughout the state.

Black crappies are common in most waters, while white crappies are abundant in the San Diego area and in the drainage basin of the Colorado River. The white catfish is the most abundant catfish in California. This species represents 95 per cent of the catfish caught in the Sacramento-San Joaquin Delta. The channel cat is the most abundant catfish in the Colorado River and is also frequently caught in the Sutter Bypass. It has also been stocked in southern California lakes. Yellow perch and walleye are present in California water but have not provided much sport for anglers.

COLORADO

Colorado Game Fish and Parks Division
6060 Broadway,
Denver 80216, Colorado

Good fishing begins in Colorado in July when the snow has runoff the slopes and the ice has gone out from the high country lakes. In this kind of country it is trout which lure out the fishermen. The High Lakes in the San Juan River Drainage Region offers native and big brook trout; the Conejos River in Conejos County is excellent for fly fishing rainbow and brown trout; and the Rio Grande River in Rio Grande County has big browns. Several newly-created lakes (or reservoirs) are presently providing exciting fishing. Steamboat Lake in Routt County and the Miramonte Reservoir, south of Norwood are two of these. The Blue Mesa Reservoir in Gunnison

County is excellent for kokanee salmon, Lake Granby also boasts this quarry. Twin Lakes near Leadville has large lake trout, known locally as Mackinaw, as have the Grand Mesa lakes east of Grand Junction. September and October are the better months for fishing in Colorado.

CONNECTICUT

State Board of Fisheries and Game
State Office Building,
Hartford 06115, Conn.

Connecticut boasts the "best shad fishing in the U.S."

The Connecticut River at the Enfield Dam does indeed attract fishermen at the end of May or early June.

There is excellent kokanee fishing to be found at the East Twin Lake, Salisbury. Framington River is good for brown and rainbow trout as is the Housatonic River, Mashapaug Lake is fine for bass, pickerel and trout, crappies, brown bullhead, bluegill, white catfish and carp. Connecticut has more than 4,000 lakes and over 300 rivers and streams covering in total some 60,000 acres.

DELAWARE

Division of Fish and Wildlife
or
Division of Parks Recreation and Forestry
Dover 19901, Delaware

Delaware, so close to New York, Atlantic City and Washington, draws sportsmen to its salt water fishing. This little state has, however, abundant largemouth bass, as well as crappie and bluegill. Pickerel is plentiful and smallmouth bass, shad and channel catfish are present. There are 50 lakes in the state, thirty-odd have public fishing access; there are 20 rivers and streams and plentiful farm ponds.

FLORIDA

Division of Game and Fresh Water Fish,
620 S. Meridian,
Tallahassee 32304, Florida

Florida is often considered as a salt-water fishing state only. Visitors should not overlook the fine freshwater angling that is available.

Largemouth bass, black crappie, channel catfish, and bluegill are all abundant. Chain pickerel, alligator gar, shad and carp are present in the state, as are redear sunfish and bream.

There are some 7,000 lakes, more than 1,500 rivers and streams, totalling 3,014,890 acres of water.

Lake Jackson, near Tallahassee, is noted for large bass. Also in the northwest, Juniper Lake, near DeFuniak Springs is recommended for bass. In central Florida, there are many good fishing lakes, including Hatchineha, Lake Tohopekaliga and Lake Kissimmee.

GEORGIA

Georgia Game and Fish Commission
Public Information Division
401 State Capitol Building
Atlanta, Ga. 30334

In Georgia there is variety in the kind of fishing and the choice of game species. A plentiful supply of water and a fine climate combine to make this a prime fishing state. The streams of north Georgia in the southern Appalachian and Blue Ridge Mountains support rainbow, brook and brown trout. These streams are stocked regularly but native fish can be found.

There are 17 major reservoirs in the state. Crappie, white bass, bluegill, redear, and redbreast sunfish are the mainstays of these large impoundments.

Bass is king in Georgia. Lake Lavier, Seminole, Walter F. George and Clark Hill are recommended for largemouth. Lakes Chatuge and Blue Ridge are notable for bronze backs. Lakes Sinclair, Clark Hill, Allatoona, and Lanier are suggested for white bass. Lakes Blue Ridge. Burton and Hartwell have established populations of walleye.

Rivers and streams in the central and south of Georgia offer Alapaha, Saltilla and Suwanee. Spawning saltwater striped bass and American shad are found in some of these rivers seasonally. The Flint River also provides fishing for a local smallmouth called the "Flint River bass".

IDAHO

Fish and Game Department
600 S. Walnut,
Box 52,
Boise 83707,
Idaho

The Idaho fisherman is fortunate. He can angle in the rivers, lakes and reservoirs of the plains and valleys, or go up to the streams and alpine lakes of the mountains. He can try for a variety of trout and salmon, or bass and pan fish.

In the Idaho Panhandle the fisherman can try Priest Lake for record trout (MacKinaw), or for rainbow and cutthroats and kokanee salmon. Pend Oreille Lake, also in the Panhandle is noted for rainbow trout. The U.S. record rainbow (Kamloops) weighing 37 lbs. was taken from this lake. Pend Oreille Lake is also fished for kokanee. The Clearwater River is a good choice for steelheads and smallmouths. The Salmon River is fished for chinook salmon and trout. Henrys Fork of the Snake River and Silver Creek are fine for trout fly fishing.

ILLINOIS

Division of Fisheries
Department of Conservation,
102 State Office Building,
Springfield, Ill. 62706

Illinois is a heavily populated state, but even so there is good fishing throughout. The fisheries division of the Department of Conservation, states "that there is no lack of fish in Illinois and that the majority of the adult fish population are not caught by anglers, but die of old age." Their records show that nearly 90 per cent of those who fish either catch only a few or no fish at all. Thus, the dedicated angler should experience little difficulty in making a satisfactory catch.

Lake Michigan provides good angling for coho from the time the ice goes out in March. Lake trout, brownies, steelheads and chinook may also be found. Try Lake Chatauqua in the Chatauqua National Wildlife Refuge for largemouth bass, crappie, bluegill and channel catfish. The 42 state conservation lakes probably provide the most outstanding fishing in Illinois; try the Chain O'Lakes area in north-eastern Illinois for northern pike, "old mossback", crappie, stripers, bluegill sunfish, channel catfish and the odd walleye. The Spring Lake conservation area is good for largemouths, crappie, bluegill and channel catfish.

The Crab Orchard National Wildlife Refuge has lakes which are good for bass, crappie, bluegill and channel cat.

The Mississippi from Rock Island to East Dubuque has good fishing for sauger, bigmouth, crappie, striped bass, bluegill, walleye and channel catfish.

INDIANA

Division of Fish and Game
608 State Office Building,
Indianapolis 46204, Indiana

The tip of Lake Michigan belongs to Indiana and there are as well, more than 1,000 lakes and reservoirs in the state along with a number of fine rivers and streams.

Fishermen seek coho in Lake Michigan beginning with the spring thaw. Indiana has stocked rainbows and chinook and coho salmon in some rivers and streams. Try the Little Calumet River, and Trail Creek.

Try for walleye in the Kankakee River and the Pigeon River for pike, smallmouth bass and trout. The muskellunge is present in Indiana but it is rare, and now protected. Try for smallmouths and northern pike in the Fawn River, and the lakes of Shakamak State Park for bass, redear, and bluegill sunfish. Crappie, bullheads catfish and carp are also abundant in the state.

IOWA

State Conservation Commission,
300-4th Street,
Des Moines 50319, Iowa

Iowa has rivers: The Mississippi and the Missouri and their tributaries, altogether some 18,000 miles of rivers and streams. As well, there are, excluding farm ponds, about 450 lakes. This agriculturally rich state is also rich in fishing waters.

The Mississippi is excellent for white bass, walleye, sauger, bluegill, largemouths and crappie. The National Lakes Region is excellent for bullheads, walleye, northern pike and yellow perch. Rainbow and brown trout are stocked in a goodly number of spring fed streams in the northeast section of the state. Muskallunge have been stocked in the Okoboji and Clear Lakes over the past several years and these fish are now being taken from these waters. Musky should be good in the future in a recently-stocked Rathbun Reservoir in southern Iowa. Smallmouth bass are to be found in a number of areas including West Okoboji Lake, Upper Iowa River and the Cedar River.

KANSAS

Forestry, Fish and Game Commission,
Box 1028,
Pratt 67124

What nature did not provide in Kansas, man has supplied. The natural lakes in Kansas are shallow bodies of water which dry up in periods of low rainfall. The various governments have, however, constructed some 177 lakes, or man-made impoundments, and these, along with about 150 rivers and streams suitable for angling, provide excellent fishing. There are as well thousands of stocked farm ponds.

The growth of fish in these stocked and controlled lakes is quite phenomenal. Waters stocked only a few years ago produce fine examples of walleye, northern pike, largemouth bass, crappies, channel catfish and more. Perry Reservoir and Glen Elder reservoir are relatively new artificial reservoirs and are expected to provide above average angling success for several years. Other areas offering similar fishing are: Kirwin, Milford, Council Grove, and Pomona reservoirs. A number of lakes provide fishing for largemouth bass, crappie, bluegill and channel catfish.

The Neosho River between St. Paul and Burlington provided the state record for catfish at 86 lbs. 3 oz. The smaller rivers and streams also yield fine catches of bass, crappie, sunfish and bull-heads.

KENTUCKY

Department of Fish and Wildlife Resources,
State Office Building, Annex,
Frankfort 40601, Kentucky

With 12 major impoundments, 41 state-owned lakes, thousands of farm ponds and rivers with more miles of running water than any other state except Alaska, it is said that fish bite every day in Kentucky.

Kentucky Lake is mentioned for crappie, bass and rainbow; and Lake Herrington for bass and rainbow trout. Lake Cumberland is good for rainbow and white bass. A smallmouth bass weighing 11 lbs. 15 oz. was taken from Dale Hollow lake in 1955. Striped bass fishing has provided real sport in the Kentucky and Cumberland Lakes as well.

There are muskies in some Kentucky rivers. Try the Green River near the Mammoth Cave. The Green River is also noted for bass. Walleye have been stocked in the Barren Reservoir and the Rough River Reservoir and the fish is doing well in these spots.

160

LOUISIANA

Louisiana Wildlife and Fisheries Commission,
400 Royal Street,
New Orleans, La. 70130

Rivers, bayous, canals and lakes provide fishing in every part of the state of Louisiana.

Crappie or sac-a-lait, largemouth and spotted bass along with bream are the most sought after species.

Fishermen will find striped bass and walleye as well in the Toledo Bend Lake. Black Lake is great and the Bussey Brake Reservoir offers fine fishing. Gizzard shad, bullheads, catfish, bluegills, carp and redear sunfish are all abundant here.

MAINE

Department of Inland Fisheries and Game
State Office Building,
Augusta 04330, Maine

This marvellous fishing state has the reputation for possessing the largest sport fishery for landlocked salmon in the world. The fish, native to Maine has been distributed throughout the state and is present in nearly 100 Maine waters. Sebago Lake, Chesuncok and Square Lake are recommended. The sea-run version of the same species, the Atlantic salmon, is also present. Originally found in some 20 rivers, the Atlantic salmon is now spawning in only nine Maine rivers. The construction of dams has probably caused the decline. Annual catch is about 400 salmon. Try rivers in Washington county. Maine is the only state in the U.S. where the sea-run Atlantic salmon can be caught.

Branch Lake near Ellsworth Maine was one of the first U.S. lakes where the brown trout was introduced and this lake is still a good one for brownies, although the fish can be found throughout the state.

All rainbow trout in Maine are resident, there are no steelhead. All of the populations present are located in streams of the Kennebuc, Androscoggin and Aroostook river basins, alhough they are being stocked elsewhere. The Bingham area of the Kennebec is recommended.

Lake trout, or togue in Maine, are to be found in deep cold-water lakes or may be found in shallow waters in the north when spawning in the late fall. Big lake trout have been taken from Moosehead Lake.

The brook trout, commonly called squaretail in Maine, is a native of the state. The Kennebago watershed in the Rangeley area, the area of the Allagash Wilderness Waterway and Lake Nesowadnehunk are mentioned for this cold water fish.

Floods is a special lake, where one can fish for the only Sunappe trout in Maine. Salmon and brookies are also present.

The smallmouth bass is important as a game fish in Maine. Good lakes for the bronze back are Scraggley and Big Lake in the east and lots of lakes in the south towards the coast. Winthrop and Belgrades lakes are recommended for largemouths. You may also fish in Maine for pickerel, lake whitefish, crappie, shad, carp and bullhead.

MARYLAND

State of Maryland, Fish and Wildlife Administration,
State Office Building,
Annapolis

Like Delaware, much fishing in Maryland is saltwater, and too often freshwater angling is overlooked. There are 25,000 acres of rivers and streams and 27,000 acres of lakes and reservoirs in this small state. Spawning shad run Maryland rivers in April and May, while the Potomac and Susquehanna rivers are most often mentioned for this fish. The upper Potomac has been stocked with smallmouth bass and produces better than average catches. Fishermen head for Deep Creek Lake for brown trout and northern pike. The Youghiogheny River presents difficult access, but good trout, and Lock Raven and Liberty Reservoirs produce fine catches of smallmouth and largemouth bass. Ponds along the eastern shore of the state are fished for bass, crappie and pickerel.

MASSACHUSETTS

Massachusetts Division of Fisheries and Game
Information and Education,
Westboro 01581, Mass.

Massachusetts's record list is an impressive one; it includes a wide variety of fish of good size. Squannacook River between Townsent and Groton and the Deerfilled River along the Mohawk trail and the Westfield River are all fine for trout fly fishing. The Connecticut River below Holyoke is for shad angling in May and early June. The Merrimack River is fished for carp as well as bass and pickerel. Nickerson State Park has waters for trout and bass. The upper Connecticut River has trout, bass and pickerel. A number of

162

reservoirs promise fishing variety; Quabbin Reservoir offers rainbow, brown and lake trout, landlocked salmon largemouth and small-mouth bass, perch, pickerel and various other panfish. Putnamville Reservoir which is not far from Boston supplies pickerel and healthy-sized bass.

MICHIGAN

Department of Natural Resources,
Fisheries Division,
Mason Building,
Lansing 48926, Michigan

Michigan controls more than 67 per cent of the total Great Lakes waters of the United States. No point in the state is more than 84 miles from one of the four bordering lakes or their connecting waters. In recent years, states and provinces bordering the Great Lakes have joined in a concerted effort to bring the sea lamprey under control and they are beginning to realize the need for environmental control to keep these magnificent inland seas in a healthy condition. The control of the lamprey is coincident with the re-surgence of lake trout and steelhead populations. The stocking of coho and chinook salmon has brought about a great rise in sport fishing in this region. Coastal areas off the towns of Pentwater, Ludington, Manistee, Onekama and Frankfort are recommended.

Chinook spawning begins in mid-September; fish for these at the southern end of Manistree Lake and in the Muskegon River from Lake Michigan to the Croton Dam. During the steelhead run in the late fall, look to the lower peninsula river, Big Manistee and Mustegon for superb catches. The most touted spot for trout is the Au Sable River system in the Lower Peninsula. Other fish sought after in Michgan are muskellunge, Northern pike, largemouth and smallmouth bass, walleye, carp, bluegill, yellow perch, (which is probably the most frequently caught game fish in Michigan), black crappie and rock bass.

MINNESOTA

State of Minnesota,
Department of Conservation,
Division of Game and Fish,
Centennial Building,
St. Paul 55101, Minn.

Walleye tops the list for most fishermen in Minnesota, while northern pike follows as a close second. Muskellunge, various bass

163

and trout are also found in the 2½ million acres of fishing water, as are bluegill, perch and catfish. Lake trout and coho salmon are taken from Lake Superior, brook trout are found in north shore streams emptying into these waters. There are some 170 lakes and they have provided fine winter and summer fishing for lakers. Smallmouth bass are also in these waters. Largemouths are most evident in the lakes of the Alexandria area.

The walleye is found in lakes such as Lake-of-the-Woods, Mille Lacs Lake, Winnibigoshish and Leeche. Pike is found throughout the state.

MISSISSIPPI

Game and Fish Commission,
Game and Fish Bldg.,
402 High Street,
Box 451,
Jackson 39205

Mississippi is another state where man-made impoundments have added vitality to the fishing scene. Some of the best angling can be found in these reservoirs.

The Ross Barnett Reservoir can be fished almost all year for bluegill, catfish and bass. Sardis, the world's largest earth filled dam on the Tallahatchie River, Enid on the Yacona and Granada on the Yalobusha all have excellent largemouth bass, crappie catfish and bluegill fishing. Pickwick is another reservoir which provides fine fishing. Eagle Lake and other lakes in the Oxbow lake region are well known spots. The Mississippi Delta, another fine fishing district is renowned for crappies. The mouths of rivers entering the Mississippi Gulf Coast may also provide some excitement for the angler.

MISSOURI

Fisheries Division,
Department of Conservation,
Box 180, Jefferson Building,
Jefferson City 65101

The State of Missouri takes its fishing seriously. With 19,000 miles of streams and rivers, 315,000 acres of reservoirs, and 474 recorded springs, the state is awash with fish-filled spots. So much so that the state claims 194 species and eight subspecies composing 25 families.

If you're after largemouth bass, Missouri is for you. Seek out Table Rock Lake in the southwestern Missouri, where experts claim the best largemouth fishing in the U.S. Secondary targets for the angler can be Bull Shoals, and Lake Taneycomo, which delivered the current state record largemout of 13 lbs., 14 oz. in January of 1969, to Marvis Bushong of Gainsville. Other species in this state include smallmouth bass, Kentucky bass, white bass, bluegill, black bull head, bowfin, Buffalo, carp, chanel and blue catfish, white and black crappies, northern pike and even muskelunge. (Muskies were introduced only recently, and four have been caught from the 110 released in Lake of the Ozarks.)

Lake Taneycomo, mentioned above, also produced the state record rainbow of 13 lbs., 14¾ ozs. to an Arkansas angler.

MONTANA

Montana Fish and Game Department,
Helena 59601, Montana

Anglers from the far and wide visit Montana, eager to test their skill in the state's seven 'Blue Ribbon Streams'. These, for the most part, are sections of large rivers which total 452 miles of fishing waters which have been chosen by the experts of the Fish and Game Department as "streams of national interest".

The fish in these streams are, of course, trout! Brown, brook and rainbow trout are all abundant. Golden, lake trout, cutthroat and dolly varden trout are also dilligently sought.

Other fishing in Montana is for mountain whitefish, yellow perch and carp, these species being abundant. Northern pike, grayling, sauger, kokanee salmon, largemouth and smallmouth bass, lake whitefish lake sturgeon and pan fish also provide pleasurable fishing. Herewith, an alphabetical list of the "Blue Streams"; The Big Hole River, from the mouth to the old dam above Divide; Flathead River, below the North and Middle Forks; Madison River, from the Graycliff access area to Quake Lake; the Missouri River, from Canyon Ferry Reservoir to Toston Dam and between Smith River and the Hauser Dam; Rock Creek, east of Missoula, from the mouth to the fork; the West Gallatin River, above Williams bridge; the Yellowstone River between Boulder River and Yellowstone Park.

NEBRASKA

Nebraska Game and Park Commission,
State Capitol Building,
Lincoln 68509, Nebraska

Fishing is a year round sport in Nebraska. The state is laced with streams, some 560 of them, and is spotted with farm ponds, lakes and reservoirs, most of them underfished.

The panhandle in the northwest is where the coldwater enthusiast heads. Here, he finds the better spots for brown and rainbow trout. The panhandle, too, has fine bass and other warm water fishing. Fishing for trout can be very rewarding in the Upper Dismal River and in the tributaries of the Loup and Niobrara Rivers in the Sand Hills. Southwest Nebraska is the "Land of Big Waters" with 10 major reservoirs, 5 smaller impoundments and 4 state lakes.

Lake McConaughy has produced state record, rainbow and brown trout, northern pike, walleye, striped bass, smallmouth bass and crappie. Some lake, some fish! Harlan County Reservoir draws fishermen for walleye, white bass, and channel catfish. In the northeast the huge Lewis and Clark lake is fished for northern pike, flathead, catfish, paddlefish and sauger. An 8 lb. 5 oz. sauger came from this lake in 1961.

NEVADA

Department of Fish and Game,
Box 10678,
Reno 85910, Nevada

When you think of Nevada, think of fishing! There are about 450 rivers and streams and approximately 40 lakes in the state and fishing is enjoyed the year round.

In northeast Nevada the more hardy types can back-pack or trail ride into some spectacular fishing opportunities. Still in the northeast but not so remote is the Wildhorse Reservoir stocked with rainbows and kokanee. Lake Pyramid in the west has cutthroat trout and sacramento perch. Lake Tahoe is fished for lake trout (mackinaw) rainbow and kokanee. The Truckee River which flows from Tahoe to Pyramid is good for rainbow trout. Lahontan Reservoir, is well liked for a variety of species from bass to chanel cats.

Close to Las Vegas in southern Nevada are Lakes Mead and Mohave. They may be fished for rainbow trout, largemouth bass, channel catfish, and crappie.

NEW HAMPSHIRE

Fish and Game Department,
34 Bridge Street,
Concord 03301, New Hampshire

The seasons of the year are well defined in New Hampshire with each season creating changes in the fishing patterns. Landlocked salmon and lake trout fishing starts when ice goes from the lakes, usually in April. The fish stay fairly shallow through the spring, go deep to flee the summer heat but may come up again as the weather cools again in the fall.

June is the best month for largemouth bass fishing. The small-mouth bass may well bite right through the summer until late September. Fly fish for trout in New Hampshire in the early autumn. Then in the winter months fish through a frozen lake for whitefish, lake trout, pickerel and perch.

Here are some of the better spots; Winnipesaukee, Squam, Sunapee and Winnisquam lakes for landlocked salmon; Newfound and Winnisquam lakes for Lake trout. Any of 119 reclaimed ponds for brook and rainbow trout (especially Robinson Pond, Martin Meadow Pond, Country Pond and Pow Wow). Great Bay for coho. Lake Wentworth and Squam for smallmouth bass. Spofford Lake for northern pike and the Merrimack River for Walleye. There are plentiful largemouth bass in most of the reclaimed ponds.

NEW JERSEY

Division of Fish, Game and Shellfisheries,
P.O. Box 1809,
Trenton 08625, New Jersey

New Jersey is a heavily populated state, however the Bureau of Fisheries Labratory has engaged in a fairly extensive stocking pro-gram and with over 1,000 lakes and 750 miles of stockable trout streams, there is good fishing to be found.

Greenwood Lake and Lake Hopatcong have good records for warmwater fish and trout. The trout, which have been stocked in these lakes are on a 'limited take' basis.

Round Valley Reservoir offers smallmouth bass and rainbow. Round Valley is a relatively new reservoir.

Farrington Lake, Palatine Lake and Union Lake (which has limited access) have produced good warmwater fish, principally largemouth bass and sunfish.

The Delaware-Raritan Canal has good warmwater fishing and is under utilized. Upstream from Trenton the Delaware River is where the fishermen congregate in late April and May for shad.

Big Flat Brook is probably the most famous trout stream in the state but try the Ken Lockwood Gorge from the end of April through to the end of November for trout fly fishing.

There is heavy trout stocking in Saxton Falls each spring but it is over utilized. Pickerel are found in South Jersey in the spring and Jersey claims, and stands by, an extraordinary record of 22 lbs. 15 oz. for a brown bullhead.

NEW MEXICO

Department of Game and Fish,
State Capitol,
Santa Fe 87501

The topography of New Mexico is exciting and dramatic in variation and the most sought after game fish are abundant. Trout and yellow perch may be fished from May to November while all other species are fished the year round.

In the north at about 12,000 feet above sea level the angler can really enjoy rainbow fishing, while in the south by the Mexican border the warm water fishing is great.

Herewith our list of recommended waters. San Juan River for trophy size brown and rainbow trout; Conches, Ute and Alamagordo Reservoirs for good channel catfish, crappie, walleye and large-mouth bass fishing; Pocos River for good brown trout fishing; Elephant Butte Reservoir for big flathead catfish; Elephant Butte and Caballor Reservoirs for white bass; Bluewater Lake for rainbow. Latir Lakes for excellent New Mexico native cutthroat fishing; Rio Grande for brown trout and the Red River for brown and rainbow trout.

NEW YORK

Department of Environmental Conservation,
Fish and Wildlife Division,
50 Wolf Road,
Albany 12201

New York State has been blessed with fine fishing waters. There are some 70,000 miles of rivers and streams and about 2,400 lakes and countless ponds. These waters have produced some marvellous sport fishing. The Finger Lakes, the Adirondacks and the Catskills, Chautauqua Lake, Lake Ontario and the St. Lawrence River are all renowned in the world of freshwater fishing.

In New York State, some 300 ponds in the remote Adirondacks have been stocked with trout, by airplane. Maps of these ponds may be purchased from the U.S. Geological Survey, Department of the Interior, Washington 20242.

Close to New York City, fish for brown trout on the west branch of the Croton River. Fish the Finger Lakes from early April for spawning rainbow. The beauty of the Thousand Islands in the St. Lawrence River and the Niagara River, as well as Lake Chautauqua make the wait for muskellunge worthwhile. Try for walleye at Oneida Lake and for lake trout at Seneca Lake. Landlocked salmon fishing has been developed at Cayuga and Schroon lakes, Lake George and the Fulton Chain. Shad come up the Hudson and Delaware Rivers to spawn each spring with the Delaware providing the most favorable angling.

The U.S. record muskellunge was taken from the St. Lawrence River in 1957. It weighed some 69 lbs., 15 oz. the U.S. record northern pike was also taken in New York State, from the Sacandaga Reservoir in Saratoga County. It weighed 46 lbs., 2 oz.

Other fish in the state include largemouth, smallmouth and white bass, chain pickerel, yellow perch, brook trout, crappies, brown bullhead, bluegill, rock bass and carp.

NORTH CAROLINA

North Carolina Wildlife Resources Commission,
Box 2919,
Raleigh 27602

At the peak of the season from mid-April into early June and then later from September through October, fishermen regularly take their largemouth bass limit and release may times the number of fish they keep. Where the brackish water gives way to fresh, excellent fishing for largemouth, bream, robin, white perch, crappie and pickerel is found. In mid-state North Carolina prime fishing is to be found at the Roanoke River's Kerr Reservoir (a reservoir which lies in both Virginia and North Carolina). Kerr is tremendous for largemouth and landlocked striped bass, again the best times are spring and fall.

The mountains of western North Carolina offer a wide variety of fishing waters. In the lower mountain valleys there are big streams and lakes rich with largemouth and smallmouth bass, bream, crappie, walleye, and white bass. "Higher up" the largemouth give way to the smallmouth, they then give way to the trout; brown trout and rainbow first and then high in the mountain ridges the cold water native brook are found.

Strangely, some of these areas which are easily accessible from large urban areas and where the cool mountain air attracts large numbers of people, there are long runs of water that are seldom fished as often as once a year. Some 1,800 miles of streams are designated as public mountain streams. Some of these controlled streams are fished on a limited-take basis. Try the two-mile stretch of trophy waters of the Nantahala River in Macon County and the eight-mile stretch of the South Mills River in Pisgah Wildlife Management Area, in Henderson and Transylvania Counties.

You may also fish in North Carolina for shad, chain pickerel, channel catfish and carp. All are abundant.

NORTH DAKOTA

State Game and Fish Department,
2121 Lovett Avenue,
Bismarck 58501

The long rolling plains of North Dakota are topped in the north along the Canadian border by heavily wooded country. One can enjoy fishing the big reservoirs and rivers of the south or take a retreat into the northern wilderness.

Favorite holes are: Garrison Reservoir for pike and walleye; Oahe Reservoir for pike, walleye and white bass; the Missouri River for pike, walleye, white bass and sauger; and Lakes Hooke, Gravel Metigoshe and Upsilon for rainbow.

Altogether there are some 38 prime trout lakes ranging from 8 to 150 acres in size. There are many smaller pike lakes, and yellow perch, goldeye, crappies, black bullhead, bluegill, carp and channel catfish are all abundant in the state.

OHIO

Recreation and Resources Commission,
Department of Natural Resources,
907 Ohio Department Bldg.,
Columbus 43215

Modern man has been hard on the Great Lakes and Lake Erie has suffered more than the others. Still, we have at last realized what damage our headlong and unthinking rush into progress can do. Lake Erie, the supposedly 'dead lake" produces perch, bass, crappie, bluegill, coho salmon, northern pike, walleye channel catfish and brown bullhead. Look for the coho in September within two miles of the Ohio shoreline, and the Bass Island area at the mouth of the Chagrin River, Conneaut Creek and the Huron River.

Muskellunge has been planted throughout the state; the Muskingum watershed lakes, Lake Cowan and Rocky Fork lake, produce this fish for the patient anglers. Near Cincinnati, the Ohio River is presently affording good fishing for sauger, catfish and bass. Trout, while not abundant are present in the state. Finally, there are a number of flood and erosion control lakes in the state which provide fine fiishing for bass, bluegill and pickerel and the power company reservoirs have good public fishing.

OKLAHOMA

Oklahoma Department of Wildlife Conservation,
1801 North Lincoln Boulevard,
Olahoma City, 37105

Reservoirs have been a boon to fishermen in many states and provinces. Oklahoma has some 40 reservoirs to go along with its spring-fed streams, its three major rivers and numerous natural lakes.

Reservoirs generally have exceptional fishing for the first five years of their existence. Decomposing, newly flooded vegatation produces a fine crop of forage fish which in turn become dinner for the fattening bass. Three reservoirs which are currently at their peak are Arbuckle, Broken Bow and Pine Creek. Lake Vanderwork is another new impoundment. Try the Canton Reservoir for walleye, Lakes Texoma and Keystones are best bets for striped bass; for northern pike head for the Carl Etling Reservoir. Channel catfish and crappie are in all major reservoirs and lakes. Bluegill and carp are abundant in the state; muskellunge, pickerel, sauger, gar, gold-eye and some rainbow trout are present. The best bet for smallmouth bass is in the streams and lakes of the southeast.

OREGON

State Game Commission
Fisheries Division,
Box 3503,
Portland 97208

Oregon brings a gleam to the eye of the salmon and steelhead fisherman. In this state in rivers such as the Rogue and the Columbia and its tributaries, the angler is challenged to pick the prime spots and to know the fish are running. They don't move on a man made schedule so it is wise to write to the State Game Commission for information regarding the anticipated spawning and sea runs. In addition to the steelheads, chinook and coho salmon, there is also a sea-run cutthroat trout.

Diamond Lake in the south has excellent rainbow trout fishing and Siltcoos Lake is a choice place for largemouth bass. In the high lakes, brook, golden and rainbow trout are sought after in the fall and the spring after the snow has gone and the trails are passable. Immense sturgeon have been taken from the Columbia and Snake Rivers. Regulations require that they be between 3 and 6 feet. Crappie, bullhead and bluegill are all abundant in Oregon. Smallmouth bass, perch, lake trout, dolly varden, mountain whitefish, channel catfish, striped bass and carp are present.

One rather remarkable lake is Hosmer Lake, formerly Mudlake, in the Deschutes National Forest. Here, one may fish for of all things, Atlantic salmon but this is 'Fish for fun' and all Atlantic salmon caught must be returned to the waters.

PENNSYLVANIA

Pennsylvania Fish Commission,
P.O. Box 1673,
Harrisburg 17102

Pennsylvania has both shared in the ravages of Lake Erie and rejoiced with other Great Lakes states and provinces in the control of the sea lamprey. Smallmouth bass, muskellunge, perch and the newly introduced coho salmon may be taken in the Presque Isle Bay area of Lake Erie.

Pennsylvania stocked some 5,828,265 trout and salmon in 1970 and 71 in 33,793 acres of streams and lakes. Stocking in 724,037 acres of warm water streams, rivers, ponds and lakes totalled 29,122,399 warmwater fry, fingerlings and adults, all of which bodes well for the future.

Fishing in the northwest and northeast corners of the state is good. In the northwest fish for largemouth bass, walleye, northern pike and muskellunge, as well as bluegill, crappies and channel catfish. In the northeast fish for walleye, chain pickerel and smallmouth bass.

The Fish Commission will send you, upon request, a pamphlet listing 100 best bass spots in Pennsylvania. Trout fishing in the state is superb. The better trout waters are in the north and the fish commission will send a list of "Favorite Pennsylvania Trout Waters". There are a number of areas open to fly fishermen only and still other areas which are 'fish for fun' spots.

The Susquehanna, above Wilkes-Barre and the Allegheny and Delaware Rivers are excellent for smallmouth bass.

172

RHODE ISLAND

Rhode Island Department of Natural Resources,
335 State Office Building,
Providence 02903

Rhode Island is, naturally enough, thought of in terms of salt water fishing. The freshwater fishing is however, really quite fine. There are 383 lakes in the state and 84 rivers and streams totalling some 25,000 acres of water.

Abundant species of fish are largemouth bass, chain pickerel, yellow perch, brown bullhead, bluegill, carp and white perch. Wood River is stocked with trout; brown, rainbow and brook, with some native brook trout present.

Smallmouth bass have been reported in 31 lakes and the Wood River. The best spots for smallmouth are Staffords' Pond, Ashville Pond, Indian Lake, Blue Pond and Worden's Pond. White perch are good at Gardiner's Pond, Herring Pond and Worden Pond.

Carp fishing at its best can be found at Mashpaug Pond, Tongue Pond, Wanskuck Pond and the Wenscott Reservoir. Other good fishing ponds in the state are; Watchmans Pond, Waterman Pond and Johnson Pond.

SOUTH CAROLINA

Wildlife Resources Commission,
Division of Game and Freshwater Fisheries,
1015 Main Street,
Box 167
Columbia 29202

Striped bass from South Carolina have been stocked in many states of the Union. The South Carolina Wildlife Resources Department has conducted an intensive research program directed toward establishing striped bass in all of the state's major reservoirs. Further, a hybrid, white bass crossed with striped bass, promises to be an exciting game fish. Lake Marion and Lake Moultrie which are connected by a diversion canal are nationally known for land-locked striped bass fishing. The spring spawning season is considered to be the best. White bass and largemouth bass are also abundant in these lakes, as are crappie and sunfish.

Trout fishing in the state is confined, with a few exceptions, to the mountainous areas of the western countries. Brown and rainbow trout are stocked in streams, in this area. Brook trout which are native to South Carolina are limited to the more remote small streams with very clear cold water. Stocking operations in South

Carolina are unannounced thus increasing the sporting atmosphere. The better fishing is to be found in the more remote areas where there is less fishing pressure. Some spots: Upper Chattooga River and Whetstone Cree, Chauga River; Whitewater River above the falls; Big Eastatoe headwater, South Saluda, from Table Rock Reservoir down; Middle Saluda River headwater, and the North Saluda River. As well there is the South Pacolet River down to the Greenville Spartanburg County line. Fishing in the Sumter National Forest is free to the public.

Pickerel, alligator gar, shad, crappie, brown bullhead, channel catfish, bluegill and carp are also abundant in the state.

SOUTH DAKOTA

Department of Game, Fish and Parks,
State Office Bldg.,
Pierre 5701

One fisherman we know, when asked to described fishing in his home state of South Dakota, threw up his hands and said "I can't, it's too good, it's good all over".

It is true that a lot of the fish most fresh water fishermen seek are abundant in this midwest state. Rainbow and brown trout are abundant in the streams of the Black Hills. Three streams most often mentioned are Spearfish, Rapid and Spring. Northern Pike are abundant in waters all over the state with the Oahe Dam being a particularly good spot. Walleye and panfish are most sought after in the northeast section of the state.

Impoundments in South Dakota generate considerable excitement. The Big Bend Dam for example, is a prime walleye lake. Other fish abundant in the state are: goldeye, white crappie, black bullhead, channel catfish, bluegill, carp, largemouth bass, white bass and yellow perch. Also present are lake sturgeon, black crappie, brown bullhead, blue catfish, redear sunfish, rock bass, smallmouth bass, sauger, kokanee salmon and brook trout.

TENNESSEE

Tennessee Game and Fish Commission,
Ellington Agricultural Center,
P.O. Box 9400
Nashville 37220

Tennessee and South Carolina have many things in common. One we know of is the development of the hybrid striped bass crossed with the white bass, a joint project of the two states' biologists. Like South Carolina, Tennessee is having tremendous success with the

174

freshwater striped bass. This bass (or rockfish) was planted in a number of Tennessee Reservoirs but has spread to almost all of the mainstream waters. The new hybrid fish is already pleasing anglers in the Cherokee and Norris Lakes.

Kentucky Lake has good largemouth bass, white crappie and channel cat fishing. Dale Hollow Reservoir has smallmouth, welleye and trout. Woods Reservoir has bass fishing and furthest south fine musky fishing. Redfoot Lake is fine for bluegill. Percy Priest Lake is another striped bass spot. Cherokee Lake is good for striped bass, white bass and crappie. Douglas Lake has largemouth bass. The Dale Hollow Tailwater, and the Little Tennessee and Hiwassee Rivers are very exciting trout streams. Plans are however, to change the Little Tennessee River into an impoundment.

TEXAS

Parks and Wildlife Department,
John H. Reagan Building,
Austin 78701, Texas

Texas has a phenomenal number of major reservoirs, 160 in all. Along with hundreds of rivers and streams the state has a total of 1½ million surface acres of fresh water.

Toledo Bend Reservoir, The Sam Rayburn Reservoir and Amistad Reservoir are all fairly new (3 to 6 years) and they are full of mature bass and crappie. The best fishing in the Sam Rayburn Reservoir is February through April. Fishing at Toledo Bend is from spring through to mid-November but it is best in the fall. The Amistad Reservoir in the Davis Mountains some 500 miles from the Toledo Bend and Sam Rayburn Reservoirs has bass, catfish and cappie and is not as heavily fished as some other lakes.

UTAH

State Department of Natural Resources,
Fish and Game Division,
1596 W.N. Temple,
Salt Lake City, 84116

There are 249 lakes and reservoirs totalling 394,182 surface acres of fresh water in Utah. Some 110,157 acres are trout waters and 283,975 acres are warm water. In addition, 612 alpine lakes and reservoirs are stocked with cutthroat and brook trout. There are 5,377 miles of streams 3,268 miles of which are trout streams.

Flaming Gorge Reservoir boasts a large trout fishing area, an enormous number of trout are taken from this lake annually. Lake Powell, the largest reservoir in Utah, has largemouth bass, walleye, channel catfish, bluegill and black crappie. The 612 alpine lakes are stocked by aircraft. They are accessable by back-packing or horse. These are located in the Uinta or Boulder Mountains in spectacular scenery. Much of the fishing in Utah is year round.

VERMONT

Fish and Game Department,
151 Main Street,
Montpelier 05602

North Vermont is peaceful and far from the stresses of urban life. Here the fisherman, if he desires, can spend quiet days in solitude.

Fish abound right through the state. There are 400 lakes, and there are 13 major watersheds made up of hundreds of streams. There are 43,000 acres of freshwater within the boundaries of Vermont plus the Vermont waters of Lake Champlain and Lake Memphremagog.

Brown, brook and rainbow trout as well as yellow perch, are the most abundant fish. Atlantic and landlocked salmon are present, as are large and smallmouth bass, muskellunge, northern pike, chain pickerel, yellow, walleye lake trout, mountain whitefish, lake sturgeon and others. Cold water lakes recommended are Willoughby, Dunmore, Caspian, Crystal, The Averills, Seymour, Echo, and St. Catharine. Warm water or combination lakes recommended are Bomoseen, Hortonia, and Burr and Huff ponds. River systems worth exploring are: Battenkill, Lamoille, White, Winooski, Missisquoi, Otter and their tributaries. Finally, there is Lake Champlain where you may catch many of the fish named above.

VIRGINIA

Salt Water Sports Fishing Association,
514 W. 25th St.,
Norfolk, 23517

The vaunted striped bass and the recently introduced muskelunge and northern pike add a special flavor to this state. The James River, in addition to the abundant smallmouth, also carry the muskies. The stripers are available both in landlocked version and sea-run. Try the Gaston, Kerr and Smith Mountain impoundments for stripers as well as the ever-popular largemouth bass. These areas are usually good in April, May and part of June as well as September through November.

All year round the striped bass can be taken by saltwater anglers in the grass flats (summer) and in the rock island of Chesapeake

Bay during the winter. The state also boasts spotted bass, chain pickerel (try Chickahominy Lake) yellow walleye, yellow perch, brook trout, brown trout, rainbows, alligator gars, white and black crappies, channel and blue catfish, bluegill and carp.

WASHINGTON
Department of Natural Resources,
General Administration Building,
Olympia 98501

The sport salmon catch averages around one million a year, with the most productive areas being at the Pacific Ocean, specifically Wesport, Ocean Shores Ilwaco and La Push. The Straits of Juan de Fuca are also enormously productive, especially around Neah Bay and Sekiu. The Puget Sound fishing is only fair, but it is expected to improve dramatically during the summer of 1972 when a 13-point Department of Fisheries program to enhance sport salmon fishing begins to show results.

Rainbow trout, steelhead, kokanee, golden trout, lake trout, cutthroat and shad in the Columbia River are also present in this state. The state claims some 51,000 lakes and 202,684 impoundments.

WEST VIRGINIA
Department of Nautral Resources,
State Capitol,
Charleston 25305

The state challenges all musky anglers to join the Husky Musky Club. The only catch is you have to land a legal-size one first, and that's 26 inches worth of fighting fish.

West Virginia's mountain streams and lakes are host to all the popular fresh water fish including smallmouth, largemouth, spotted bass, brookies, rainbow, brown trout, walleye, white bass, black and white crappies, bluegill, channel catfish, and striped bass.

The best smallmouth streams are the Shenandoah, South Branch of the Potomac, Greenbrier, and Little Kanawha Rivers. Trout fishermen rate the Cranberry, Williams, South Branch of the Potomac, North Fork of the South Branch, Shavers Fork of the Cheat and the Elk River near Webster Springs as excellent. Nearly 200 lakes and streams are stocked with various trout.

Crappies anglers should choose Bluestone, Sutton and Summersville Lakes For Walleyes, there's Greenbrier, Gauley, New and Elk

Rivers. The omnipresent channel catfish inhabit most of the warm water lakes and rivers as well as the state-controlled impoundments.

WISCONSIN

Department of Natural Resources,
Box 450, Madison 53701

With 5,093 named lakes, 35,000 miles of rivers and streams, totalling 909,333 acres, you would think Wisconsin had enough water. Nope. The Great Lakes provide access to some of the best inland fishing in the country. Authorities there report a "spectacular improvement" in fishing as a result of salmon stocking. Look to the northern third of the state to provide the best fishing border to border. There's musky fishing as good as any place in the continent save perhaps the St. Lawrence River, and recent stockings have sent coho and chinooks into the area. The state also provides all the standard freshwater fish including the largemouth and smallmouth bass, black and white crappies, perch, bluegills, bullheads and a wide variety of catfish.

For muskies look at Bolder Junction or Lake Chippewa, Lac Vieux Desert and North Twin Lake.

The Mississippi River provides a wide mixture of fishing for the angler including everything save muskies and trout.

WYOMING

Game and Fish Commission,
Box 1589
Cheyenne

High mountain waters to big rivers, over 7,000 miles of them that's the fishing in this romantic state. Brown trout, that canny German import, is one of the main attractions of this place, in addition to golden, lake trout, splake, rainbow steelhead, mountain whitefish and the warmer water species, black crappies, black bullheads, channel cats, bluegill, pumpkinseed, carp and rock bass.

The North Platte River is probably the best for brown trout and rainbow, although the Green River and the Flaming Gorge Reservoir run a close second. The Bridger Wilderness area is a place all its own for the trout mentioned. There's also the Snake River, its tributaries, and Jackson Lake.

For the beautiful golden, try Alpine Lake in the Wind River Indian Reservation.

ALBERTA

Alberta Government Travel Bureau
Department A5
Highways Building,
Edmonton, Alta.,

Alberta is prairies, cow country, rolling foothills, and magnificent mountains, with alpine lakes accessible only by foot or horseback. Alberta is remote northern wilderness with lakes where you can pick and choose your trophy fish.

Tyrrell Lake south of Lethbridge is an impoundment stocked, through a cooperative government venture, with 1,400,000 rainbow fingerlings. The highest expectations for this lake have been surpassed. Equally pleasing, another man-made impoundment, Chain Lake provides exciting rainbow fishing, along with dolly vardens and cutthroats. The northern pike is fished throughout the province but is especially good in the southern part. Seven lakes in the northern regions have been designated as trophy lakes. In three of these, Gods Lakes, May Lake and Seibert Lake, the limit is two pike and six walleye per day, but you can catch and release until you are exhausted, keeping your favorites. Andrew, Gardiner, Namur and Winefred Lakes are also trophy lakes. In the far north Indian guides can provide exciting trips; arrangements are made through the government offices.

Cold Lake on the Saskatchewan border has been well stocked with coho salmon and it also has other fish.

There are five National Parks in the rocky Mountain Range. The ice does not go out of the high alpine lakes until the late spring, or early June. Many of these lakes can only be reached by backpacking or trail rides, but they provide exciting fishing in a beautiful peaceful setting.

BRITISH COLUMBIA

Fish and Wildlife Branch
Department of Recreation and Conservation
Parliament Buildings
Victoria, B.C.

There are 10,000 lakes, countless rivers and streams amidst 266,266 square miles of mountains, farmland, forests and desertland in British Columbia, Canada's most westerly province.

Trout are the most important freshwater fish in B.C. The rainbow is native to the province but the department of fisheries has boosted the population by adding thousands of eggs and fry over the past 50 years. Areas recommended for rainbow are the Kootenay and Okanagan lakes, the Kamloops district the Quesnel-Chilcotin district, Burns Lake in the central interior of B.C., the sea-access lakes, and many rivers and streams of Vancouver Island.

Steelhead are most often fished in the winter months after the fall and winter rains. The Queen Charlotte Islands, the Thompson River, the Kispiox and the Cowichan River on Vancouver Island, the Vedder River and the Bella Coola are a few of hundreds which could be named for superb steelhead fishing. Try the Campbell and Skeena rivers for chinook, and if you should take one over 30 lbs. you can call it a Tyee. Fish for coho in August and September in coastal waters. Coho spawn late, but they're pernickety feeders once they enter the spawning streams.

Other important game fish in B.C. are coastal cutthroat which occur in lakes and streams along the entire B.C. coast. Cutthroat are also found in southeastern B.C. in some lakes and most streams of the East Kootenays, in the Mabel Lake area and around Nelson and Revelstoke.

Brown Trout are well established on the east coast of Vancouver Island. In the upper reaches of the Cowichan, trout up to 5 lbs. have been taken. Dolly varden and lake trout are native to B.C. The lake trout is found in all the larger lakes from Shuswap north to lakes of the Yukon River drainage area. The dolly varden is spread throughout a large part of the province. Sea run variety are more plentiful toward the north coast. In the interior dolly varden inhabit the Thompson and North Thompson rivers. They are also present on Vancouver Island and in most lakes, rivers and streams open to the Fraser River.

The brook trout is present in rivers on Vancouver Island, in lakes and streams in the southeastern part of the province and around the Princeton and lower Okanagan regions.

The Arctic grayling is to be found in the farmost north of B.C., in lakes and streams of the Yukon and Peace River systems. The Montana grayling can be caught in the southeastern corner of the province. Large and smallmouth bass and yellow perch are also present in the province.

British Columbia offers fishing to satisfy almost every soul and, the entire province is breathtakingly beautiful.

MANITOBA

Department of Tourism and Recreation
Department M5,
405 Norquay Building,
401 York Avenue,
Winnipeg 1, Man.

The licence plates on Manitoba automobiles declare, "Manitoba, 100,000 lakes". It is a huge province. There are certainly over 38,000 lakes and some 1,400 rivers and streams with over 39,225 square miles of water.

The north is where the real fishing is found. Here is a list of the most highly praised fishing spots in Northern Manitoba. Gods Lake for brook trout, pike, lake trout, walleye with lots of trophy fish present. Sasaginnigak Lake for pike and walleye. Eagle Nest Lake: good pike, walleye, and excellent smallmouth bass. Lake Athapapuskow for big lake trout. Other fish found in Manitoba are sauger, yellow perch, kokanee salmon, grayling. Arctic char, rainbow trout, lake whitefish (abundant throughout the north), goldeye, lake sturgeon, crappy, bullhead, channel catfish, bluegill carp and rock bass.

ONTARIO

Department of Tourism and Information
185 Bloor Street East
Toronto 285

Ontario boasts more than a quarter-million lakes, an equal number of rivers and streams, and about 25 per cent of the world's fresh water. Muskies approaching the world record have been taken from such widely-dispersed bodies of water as Lake of the Woods on the western border to the St. Lawrence River below the eastern boundaries.

Lake Nipissing, Lake Nosbonsing, the French River and the Kawartha Lakes regularly yield trophy fish, and Georgian Bay between Parry Sound and Midland is unsurpassed anywhere. Best time to tie into one of these freshwater "sharks" is from early September until mid-November.

Pike abound across the length and breadth of Ontario's 415,000 square miles of water and wilderness.

Largemouth bass angling is confined to the south-eastern region, with the Kawarthas, Rideau Lakes, and Land 'o' Lakes the prime producers.

Smallmouth angling is good throughout the Great Lakes, and great in most of the lakes and rivers of north-western Ontario. Mounting-size brook trout inhabit most of the rivers of the Arctic watershed — those flowing northward into James and Hudson Bay — with Algonquin Park, Foote Lake near Chapleau, andthe famed Nipigon River and Lake all producing frequent winners.

Rainbow trout are tops in the rivers which flow into Georgian Bay between Owen Sound and Port Severn, as well as on Manitoulin Island. Most of the Lake Superior waterways offer outstanding steelhead fishing too. Best times are May, October and November. There are also fantastic lake trout, coho and walleye fisheries.

It's estimated you would have to live 700 years to spend a day fishing each of Ontario's lakes, and you could figure on fillets for every meal.

THE MARITIME PROVINCES OF CANADA

New Brunswick,
Department of Fisheries,
Fredericton

Nova Scotia,
Department of Lands and Forests,
Halifax

Prince Edward Island,
Fish and Wildlife Division,
Charlottetown, P.E.I.

The most important thing to say about these three provinces which form the eastern bulwark of Canada is atlantic salmon. For it is here that the king of the salmon is found, fighting its way majestically up the famous salmon rivers such as the Mersey, The Medway, the Margaree in Nova Scotia; the Mirimichi, the Restigouche, Dungarvon, and Big Salmon rivers of New Brunswick; the Mill, Dunk, West and Vernon rivers of Prince Edward Island.

Restrictions on seasons and method of catch here are strict to protect this much-sought-after beauty. Anglers from across North America and Europe have come to this area for atlantic salmon. In 1970 in New Brunswick's southwest Mirimichi River alone, more than 20,000 atlantic salmon were landed. Although Atlantic salmon provide enormous tourist appeal, the lakes and rivers are filled with a variety of other species. In New Brunswick, there are many small-mouth bass, landlocked salman and lake trout, brook and brown trout and brown bullheads. In Nova Scotia's 3,000 plus lakes and 100 rivers, the angler finds brown, rainbow and speckled trout, chain pickerel, smallmouth bass and the inevitable yellow perch. They are particularly proud of Lake Ainslie where 3-4 pound speckled can be landed.

Prince Edward Island, a tiny gem of an island quite unique unto itself, boasts in addition to atlantic salmon, brook, Kamloops and steelhead, striped bass and white perch. With only 10 natural lakes anda dozen major rivers, this small lovely secluded hideaway from the world does not boast trophy angling, but has everything else to offer the angler. PEI is also known for its tuna runs, with average 740 pound blue fins steaming by the eastern tip on the great Gulf current.

NEWFOUNDLAND

Tourist Development Office, or
Department of Mines, Agriculture and Resources,
Confederation Building,
St. John's

A fascinating boat-ride or a short air hop away, the island of Newfoundland offers great fishing for Atlantic salmon, landlocked salmon, brookies, brown trout and rainbows. Try the Granite and Pudhops lakes for 15-pound landlocked or healthy brook trout. Rainbows are only in stocked ponds. The Atlantic salmon, some-what depleted by commercial fishing, still make spectacular runs up the rivers, notably Gray River, Gander River and River of Ponds. Again fly-fishing only for these beauties. In the still-rugged, lonely and isolated Labrador on the mainland, Arctic char, fabulous brook trout, lake trout, northern pike, and splake or wendigo, fill the lakes and rivers, as well as Atlantic salmon on the coast.

For brookies try Lake Tasuiyak or Little Minipi Lake for lake trout try along the Churchill River, and for Arctic char any of the foregoing should be good.

In this still undeveloped area, many anglers use charters to get into isolated lakes and rivers in the absence of roads. Some fly direct from spots in the northern U.S., while many local jaunts can be planned from Goose Bay.

QUEBEC

Department of Tourism, Game and Fish,
Parliament Buildings,
Quebec City

This province expansively announces it has more than 1,000,000 lakes, rivers and streams totalling more than 300,000 square miles, or about half the entire territory. And what fishing!

From Arctic char and speckled trout on the lip of Hudson Bay to the mighty muskelunge in the St. Lawrence River and the Atlantic salmon in the Gaspe Peninsula, Quebec is *formidable.*

The Fort George Indian Association on James Bay runs exciting fishing and hunting trips along the coast. Book early for this one, say about a year in advance, and spend hours on the Seal and Roggan Rivers landing lunker speckeled and Arctic char. Quebec is threatened by the gigantic James Bay power development scheme which critics say will upset the ecology of the area. A few years may see the angling dramatically changed in this incredibly beautiful northern angling spot.

Elsewhere in the province, the Atlantic salmon run in the Matane River is one of life's precious moments. Although endangered recently by the Danish and Norwegian commercial fisheries, the Atlantic salmon also runs in rivers in the North Shore and at Ungava Bay, in the George and Whale rivers.

In the Eastern townships, south of Montreal, the angler will find the best rainbow, brown trout, perch, chain pickerel, and small-mouth bass. Around Montreal itself the giant muskellunge and the northern pike hold sway in the St. Lawrence River.

The vast province still has many undiscovered lakes (undiscovered by the angler, that is) in the great north, and speckled trout, Quebec red trout, walleye, landlocked salmon, lake whitefish and Arctic char abound. A number of areas in Quebec are still under licence to private fishing clubs, so checking with the Department of Tourism before heading here is wise. Many of the remote fishing spas are reachable by air charters.

SASKATCHEWAN

Province of Saskatchewan,
Department of Natural Resources,
Fisheries & Wildlife Branch,
Provincial Office Building,
Prince Albert, Saskatchewan

Fishing yarns fall easily from the lips of the Saskatchewan fisherman. This province is immense, its lakes and rivers are almost countless and you can fish just about anywhere. The real enthusiast, though, heads north. A Saskatchewan fisherman might say, "The cold, clear lakes of the north breed the biggest, fightingest, tastiest fish you've ever seen."

Some choice spots for the enthusiastic fisherman, then, would be as follows: Northern Pike: Cree Lake; Geikie River (Wollaston Lake); Churchill River; Lac la Ronge; Amisk Lake; Saskatchewan River; Diefenbaker Lake.

Walleye: Churchill River; Dore Lake; Saskatchewan River; Last Mountain Lake; Lac la Ronge. Lake Trout: Lac la Ronge; Whelan Bay; Wollaston Lake; Cree Lake; Waterbury Lake; Black Lake; Tazin Lake.

Grayling: Fond du Lac River; Clearwater River; Cree River; Wollaston Lake; Reindeer Lake. Sturgeon: Saskatchewan River; Churchill River.

Brown: the streams of the Cypress Hills, with Bone Creek being noteworthy. Rainbow: Piprell Lake. Brook: Streams of the Cypress Hills in the south-west; Fir River and Little Amyot, and Sealey Lakes.

Wendigo (Splake): Lakes Baldy and Burtlein. Goldeye: Saskatchewan River. Perch: throughout the province, with the Qu'Appelle Lakes, Kenosee Lake, Duncairn Dam, Struthers Lake, Jackfish and Murray Lakes all producing immense quantities of this species.

Visitors to Saskatchewan should be aware that distances in the Canadian north are great. Many of these northern spots mentioned have fishing camps and special fly-in charters. Prospective fishermen should write to the department listed above for information, well in advance of any possible trip.

YUKON AND NORTHWEST TERRITORIES

Yukon,
Department of Fisheries
and Department of Travel and Information,
Dept. Y5, Whitehorse

Northwest Territories,
Travel Arctic, Dept. NT5,
Yellowknife, NWT

The Yukon and Northwest Territories, are enormous. Nothing written in these short paragraphs could begin to prepare a visitor for the fishing adventures awaiting him.

The angling season is obviously shorter than in the south but then trolling deep for large lake trout is rarely necessary. Large pike seeking warm water can be taken from shallow side channels and bays of large lakes. The fish really do come big up here. A 5 lb. 15 oz. Arctic grayling came from a tributary of Great Bear Lake. The record northern pike from the Northwest Territories is over 41 lbs. The record rainbow trout in the Yukon Territories is 19 lbs. 2 oz. Here, 25 lb. lake trout are not uncommon. Arctic char is another exciting fish caught regularly. The record in the N.W.T. is 28 lbs. 2 oz.

Flying is the general method of moving about. The people are warm, the terrain fantastic. Write to the above departments for information and then go and enjoy yourself.

Index